Harley Granville Barker

Twayne's English Authors Series

Kinley E. Roby, Editor
Northeastern University

TEAS 309

*Granville Barker, photographed by
Bernard Shaw at Shaw's home, Ayot
Saint Lawrence.*

Harley Granville Barker

By Elmer W. Salenius

Framingham State College

Twayne Publishers · Boston

82-1023

Harley Granville Barker

Elmer W. Salenius

Copyright © 1982 by G. K. Hall & Company
All Rights Reserved
Published by Twayne Publishers
A Division of G. K. Hall & Company
70 Lincoln Street
Boston, Massachusetts 02111

Book Production by John Amburg
Book Design by Barbara Anderson

Printed on permanent/durable acid-free
paper and bound in the United States of
America.

Library of Congress Cataloging in Publication Data

Salenius, Elmer W. (Elmer William)
  Harley Granville Barker.

  (Twayne's English authors series;
TEAS 309)
  Bibliography: p. 146
  Includes index.
  1. Granville-Barker, Harley, 1877–1946
—Criticism and interpretation.
I. Title. II. Series.
PR6013.R29Z86   1982   792'.0924   82-8493
ISBN 0-8057-6801-7   AACR2

To My Wife

Contents

About the Author

A native of Massachusetts, Elmer William Salenius graduated from Boston University College of Liberal Arts, received the A.M. degree from Harvard Graduate School of Arts and Sciences and his Ph.D. from Boston University. His interest in the theater began in childhood, when he delighted in accompanying his mother to rehearsals of the amateur productions in which she appeared prominently, and this interest has remained strong. He taught at the American University in Shrivenham, England, and at Boston University before joining the faculty at Framingham State College, where for many years he has taught courses in modern drama, Shakespeare, and British literature, and has served as chairman of the English Department.

Preface

Today most people who recognize the name Harley Granville Barker probably associate him with his prefaces to Shakespeare's plays, which have appeared in various editions, both hardcover and paperback, and which ensure him a lasting place in the history of Shakespeare criticism. From the turn of the century to the time of World War I, however, Barker achieved considerable success as an actor, particularly in plays by Shaw; and he gained a wide reputation as an outstanding producer of the "new" drama and of Shakespeare. He did much to establish the producer in place of the actor-manager as the artistic director of the play. Under the Vedrenne-Barker management of the Court Theatre from 1904 to 1907 Shaw's reputation as a dramatist was established, and the works of many other new English and continental dramatists were introduced to London. Indeed this Court Theatre venture is now regularly referred to as one of the most significant in the history of British drama. A few years later Barker extended his fame through a series of Shakespeare revivals which were outstanding in their fidelity to the text of the plays, and in the speed, simplicity, and beauty of the productions.

Besides being an actor and a producer, Barker was also a dramatist. Though his plays were not universally praised by the critics nor extremely popular with audiences, most of them were produced with some measure of success and have lasting interest and value in both method and content. Indeed Bernard Shaw felt that Barker the dramatist had been unjustly neglected. In "Barker's Wild Oats," which he wrote after Barker's death in 1946, Shaw calls Barker's plays "treasures to be preserved."[1]

After Barker's retirement from active work in the theater his contributions as a lecturer and a critic showed his continued interest in the drama and gave him an honored place in the academic world.

This study is concerned with Barker's work related to the theater and the drama. I say nothing about the few things he wrote that have no connection with his major activities as actor, producer, dramatist, and critic, though they are listed in the bibliography. I do not comment on any of his unpublished writings, nor on his translations and adaptations of some twenty plays by continental dramatists, mainly Spanish. The first chapter describes, as part of a brief biographical sketch, Barker's work as an actor. The second deals with his career as a producer. Though I have made no attempt to mention every play he produced, I have included his most important accomplishments in this field. The several chapters following present in chronological order an analysis of Barker's eight original long plays (including two collaborations) and his three one-act plays, with a general chapter on his work as a dramatist. The final chapter comments on Barker's chief ideas and contributions as a critic.

I hope to have provided a comprehensive survey of Barker's work in the theater and an analysis of his writings, giving a fairly detailed picture of the various interrelated spheres of his activity. I trust that this study will increase the reader's knowledge and appreciation of the accomplishments of this most versatile and talented man of the theater.

Elmer W. Salenius

Framingham State College

Acknowledgments

I express my thanks to The Society of Authors as the literary representatives of the Estate of Harley Granville-Barker and to Sidgwick & Jackson, Publishers, for permission to quote from the works of Barker; and to Associated Book Publishers Ltd. for permission to quote from Barker's *The Madras House.* I am also grateful to The Society of Authors on behalf of the Bernard Shaw Estate for permission to quote from Shaw's published works and from an unpublished letter from Shaw to me, and to use as the frontispiece of this book a photograph of Barker taken by Shaw, which he kindly sent to me. In addition to Shaw, the late Walter Hampden was most gracious in answering my questions about Barker. I also acknowledge with appreciation my indebtedness to various other sources which are cited in the notes and bibliography.

I wish to thank Dr. D. Justin McCarthy, president of Framingham State College, and the Trustees of the Massachusetts State Colleges for allowing me a semester's sabbatical leave in order to finish this book. I am grateful to my colleagues in the English Department at Framingham State College for assuming my teaching load in my absence, and especially to Dr. William E. Sellers, who took over the duties of the chairmanship of the department. I thank also Ms. Laurel Bisson, who typed the manuscript and gave me the benefit of her skill and knowledge. Finally, I thank my wife, Frances, without whose encouragement this work would never have been completed.

Chronology

of Barker's lifelong interest in the establishment of a national theater. December 23, first performance of *Prunella* by Laurence Housman and Barker, at the Court.

1905   November 7, first performance of *The Voysey Inheritance*, at the Court.

1906   April 24, Barker and Lillah McCarthy married.

1907   November 24, private performance of Barker's *Waste*, which was refused a license for public performance. A so-called public performance (actually a reading) was given on January 28, 1908, with cuts required by the censor.

1910   March 9, first performance of Barker's *The Madras House*, at the Duke of York's.

1911   March 11, first performance of Schnitzler's *Anatol* in Barker's English version with Barker in the leading role. Beginning of the Lillah McCarthy-Granville Barker management of the Little Theatre, and Barker's final public appearance as an actor in London.

1912   September 21, his production of *The Winter's Tale* opens at the Savoy. November 15, his production of *Twelfth Night* opens.

1914   February 6, his production of *A Midsummer Night's Dream* opens.

1915   January 28, first of a series of productions in New York: *Androcles and the Lion* and Anatole France's *The Man Who Married a Dumb Wife* on a double bill, followed by *A Midsummer Night's Dream* and *The Doctor's Dilemma*. Develops friendship with Helen Huntington, a poet and novelist. Writes *The Red Cross in France*.

1916   August, enlists in the Royal Horse Artillery.

1917   January, in America for a series of lectures. April 19, divorces Lillah McCarthy. Long short story *Souls on Fifth*.

1918   July 31, marries Helen Huntington.

1921   January 8, first performance in London of his last full-scale production, Maeterlinck's *The Betrothal*.

1922   *The Exemplary Theatre*.

1923   *The Secret Life*.

1927   First of five series of Shakespeare *Prefaces*.

1928   Last play, *His Majesty*.

1930   *A National Theatre*, a rewriting of *Scheme and Estimates for a National Theatre*. Gives Clark Lectures at Trinity College, Cambridge, published as *On Dramatic Method*. Settles in Paris.

1933   May 3, supervises first performance of revised version of *The Voysey Inheritance*.

1936   Fall, *Waste* produced at Westminster Theatre. Barker named on program as co-producer with Michael MacOwan.

1940   Spring, assists Lewis Casson in production of *King Lear* at the Old Vic, with Gielgud. September, settles in New York. During war years lectures at Toronto University, Harvard, and Princeton.

1946   Spring, returns to Paris. August 31, dies in Paris of arteriosclerosis.

Chapter One
Introduction: Man of the Theater

According to Bernard Shaw, when he once urged Granville Barker to get on with his playwriting, Barker said, "Writing is easy for you: it is your profession; but it is not mine: I went on the stage when I was 14."[1] Indeed from his earliest appearance as an actor in 1891 until World War I, Barker's life was centered almost entirely around the theater, though not only as a performer. After first making a reputation as an actor, he soon added producing and playwriting to his accomplishments. He became a truly outstanding producer (or director, in American terminology) and a dramatist of significance. After his second marriage and his withdrawal from active work in the theater (to the great disappointment of most of his friends and associates), he still devoted himself largely to writing about the drama and the theater, achieving recognition as a scholar-critic especially for his *Prefaces to Shakespeare,* for which he is most widely known today. His work in one area undoubtedly influenced his work in the others. All of his activities show similar characteristics—a subtle intellectual quality rather than strong passion, a sincerity of approach, a serious purpose, and a high degree of accomplishment. Indeed Barker is one of the most important figures of the dramatic renaissance which came about in England with the influence of Ibsen in the latter part of the nineteenth century and which is seen in the work of Shaw, Galsworthy, Barrie, and others in the early twentieth century.

Born at Campden Hill, Kensington, London, on November 25, 1877, Harley Granville Barker came of Scottish and Italian ancestry, with a little Portuguese blood as well.[2] His father was Albert James Barker, a kind of architect; his mother was Mary Elisabeth Bozzi-Granville, the granddaughter of an Italian physician who had settled in London and changed his name from Bozzi to Granville. She was a professional reciter and bird mimic. From her Barker learned the art of speaking and reciting, for he toured with her, doing public recitations of poems, including in time passages from Shakespeare. His first public appearance in a play was in 1891 at the Spa Rooms at Harrogate as an emergency replacement in a company of juveniles.

Barker's formal academic education ended at the age of thirteen when he entered Miss Sarah Thorne's combined dramatic school and stock company at the Theatre Royal, Margate. For six months he was in Miss Thorne's company; his first appearance with her was at Margate in Wilkes's *Ben the Bo'sun*. In 1892 he was introduced by Charles Brookfield to Charles Hawtrey, who gave him the part of the Third Young Man in Brookfield's musical *The Poet and the Puppets*, in which Barker made his first appearance on the London stage. After acting with various touring stock companies (A. B. Tapping's, Lewis Waller's, and others), he toured with Ben Greet in productions of Shakespeare and Marlowe. It was in Greet's company that he met actress Lillah McCarthy, whom he later married. He also appeared in small roles with the renowned Mrs. Patrick Campbell. In 1899 he played Shakespeare's Richard II in William Poel's production for the Elizabethan Stage Society, and in 1903 he appeared in the title role in Poel's production of Marlowe's *Edward II*, both performances being highly praised.

During these early years the young Barker met several individuals who became his good friends and who influenced his development—classical scholar Gilbert Murray, critic and playwright William Archer, actors Charles Charrington and Janet Achurch (Mrs. Charrington), and Bernard Shaw; and he became closely associated with the Stage Society, an organization interested in presenting the "new" drama. Probably through the influence of the Charringtons and Shaw (twenty-one years older than Barker, a drama critic and already the author of *Plays: Pleasant and Unpleasant*), he was converted to Socialism and joined the Fabian Society in 1901. Barker's interest in politics and his belief that the living conditions of the masses must be improved before art and culture can be honestly appreciated by the élite are reflected in many of his plays. His association with the Stage Society shows that very early in his career he was already interested in the intellectual drama and in the improvement of the theater in

England. The program and spirit of the Stage Society—its interest in plays by new English dramatists and continental writers and its sympathy with the idea that the theater can be a force for the improvement of society—were in keeping with Barker's own. Acting, producing, and writing for the Society, he became one of its leading figures.

In its 1901—1902 season the Stage Society presented the first of Barker's plays written (in 1899) by him alone, *The Marrying of Ann Leete*. Before this he had already made his beginning as a dramatist in collaboration with Herbert (Berte) Thomas, a young actor (nine years older than Barker) whom he had met at Margate in Miss Thorne's company. Together they wrote five plays, only one of which, "The Weather-hen," was professionally produced (in 1899). None of the five has been published, and only three of them ("The Weather-hen," "The Family of the Oldroyds," and "Our Visitor to Work-a-Day") survive in typescript. As a dramatist Barker went on to write five more original full-length plays—*The Voysey Inheritance, Waste, The Madras House, The Secret Life*, and *His Majesty*, plus three one-act plays—*Rococo, Vote by Ballot*, and *Farewell to the Theatre*. He collaborated with Laurence Housman on *Prunella* and with Dion C. Calthrop on *The Harlequinade*. He also made numerous adaptations and translations of foreign plays.

Meanwhile, to return to Barker's earlier years, out of an invitation to produce *The Two Gentlemen of Verona* at the Court Theatre, where J. H. Leigh, with J. E. Vedrenne as manager, was giving a series of Shakespeare revivals, grew the Vedrenne-Barker management of the Court Theatre, which lasted from October 18, 1904, to June 29, 1907—one of the most significant periods in the history of the British theater. The production of *The Two Gentlemen*, with Barker playing the part of Launce, was, incidentally, a notable success.

Before the Vedrenne-Barker management proper at the Court, Barker appeared in a series of six matinee performances of Shaw's *Candida* (in which he had already played for the Stage Society), which was then repeated during the regular seasons. Shaw has described Barker at this time in words of high praise. He had been looking about, Shaw says, for an actor suitable for the part of the poet in *Candida* for the Stage Society performance and had discovered him "in a very remarkable person named Harley Granville-Barker. . . . He had a wide literary culture and a fastidiously delicate taste in every branch of art. He could write in a difficult and too precious but exquisitely fine style. He was self-willed, restlessly industrious, sober, and quite sane. He had Shakespeare and Dickens at his finger ends. Altogether the most distinguished and incomparably the most cultivated person whom circumstances had driven into the theatre at that time." Barker's appearance as Marchbanks was a high point in his career as an actor. Of it Shaw says, "His performance of this part—a very difficult one to cast—was, humanly speaking, perfect."[3] Desmond MacCarthy suggests that Barker was so successful as Marchbanks "because the representation of a lyrical mood is one within the peculiar range of his powers," and goes on to praise his voice especially: "His voice, too, can express a contemplative ecstasy. It possesses a curious individual quality, which, while it limits the range of his impersonations, gives particular intensity to some. When he repeats her name 'Candida, Candida, Candida,' there is not a touch of self-consciousness in the musical reiteration; he does not appear to be following the sound of his own voice like most actors at such times, but to be listening, detached, to his longing made audible." MacCarthy also indicates that Barker had a special talent for portraying intellectual emotions and therefore was an excellent Marchbanks.[4]

Other parts which Barker played at the Court were the Henchman in Euripides' *Hippolytus* (in which his "delivery of the messenger's speech was the most memorable feature. . . ," says MacCarthy),[5] Keegan in *John Bull's Other Island*, Pierrot in *Prunella* (by Laurence Housman and Barker), Her Lover in *How He Lied to Her Husband*, Valentine in *You Never Can Tell*, John Tanner in *Man and Superman* (he was made up with a red beard to resemble Shaw), Ekdal in *The Wild Duck*, Adophus Cusins in *Major Barbara*, Edward Voysey in his own *The Voysey Inheritance*, and Dubedat in *The Doctor's Dilemma*.[6] He also acted Henry Trebell in his own *Waste* in a Stage Society production and General Burgoyne in *The Devil's Disciple* at the Savoy and the Queen's Theatre during the 1907–1908 season.

John Tanner was one of Barker's best parts, according to MacCarthy[7] and also according to Geoffrey Whitworth, who, looking back upon Barker's career in 1948, says this performance stands out and is "most memorable for its magnificent cut-and-thrust with Lillah McCarthy as Ann Whitfield."[8] A. B. Walkley, too, has words of high praise for Barker in this characterization. He says: "Never was playwright more lucky in finding a born interpreter of his talent than Mr. Shaw in the case of Mr. Granville Barker. He is so alert, so exuberant, so 'brainy,' so engagingly impudent, so voluble in his patter."[9] As Dubedat, MacCarthy feels that Barker "suggested perfectly the character of a rather agreeably uppish, slouching, loose young blackguard at the dinner; and he dies well."[10] Barker as Father Keegan did not succeed completely, thinks MacCarthy, "in inspiring the sense of remote dignity which it is important to emphasize in contrast to the eupeptic irreverence of Broadbent and to the squalid go-as-you-please Irish character."[11] Hesketh Pearson, however, says Barker was much more effective as Father Keegan than as Tanner.[12] In *The Wild Duck*, too, Barker apparently was not completely successful. Although it was, according to MacCarthy, "an accomplished and consistent piece of acting," yet it was "too good-natured" an interpretation. "His Hjalmar Ekdal was a pitiable and ridiculous figure, instead of a repulsive and ridiculous one."[13] As Valentine in *You Never Can Tell*, Barker was fine. He excelled "in those brisk leaps of the heart, which are so characteristic of Mr. Shaw's lovers. . . ."[14] As Pierrot, too, Barker was well cast. Whitworth remembers this as one of the high points of Barker's acting career;[15] Max Beerbohm says that Barker's impersonation was "flawlessly good" and comments on the fact that Barker was not embarrassed by acting fantasy.[16]

Basically, though, it was in the new style of acting that Barker was recognized as masterful—an untheatrical, realistic style which Barker as a producer insisted on. Shaw describes Barker's style of acting as "low toned."[17] This low-toned style Beerbohm objected to in Barker's performance of General Burgoyne in *The Devil's Disciple*, in which he disliked the "plaintive monotone" of Barker's voice.[18]

Actually there are conflicting comments on Barker's voice. Frank A. Swinnerton says that it lacked resonance.[19] Yet another contemporary commentator finds his voice to be most effective. In his charm, states this writer, "he is aided by his voice, with its haunting, half-mocking intonations, and its power of suggesting unutterable things. Indeed—if we might hazard the fancy—it is in his voice that

Mr. Barker's spirit has its habitation. There lies the central essence of his individuality, the subtle secret of his charm."[20] Felix Aylmer, who appeared in two of Barker's Shakespeare productions, reports that in later life Barker felt that he had been limited as an actor by his voice, but Aylmer disagrees, saying, "His voice was not strong, but this weakness did not prevent his mastery of a wide variety of pitch and intonation."[21]

In evaluating Barker as an actor, one must conclude that though he does not rank with the immortals like Garrick or Irving in the history of the English stage, he had intelligence, subtlety, and charm, and portrayed heroes of intellectual passion, like Shaw's and his own, exceedingly well.

During his association with the Court Theatre Barker made a name for himself as a producer as well as an actor. Except for Shaw's works (which were produced by the dramatist himself), Barker produced all of the plays presented at the Court. His work as a producer will be commented on in more detail in the next chapter. Suffice it to say here that the Vedrenne-Barker seasons at the Court Theatre are recognized as a high point in the history of the English stage.

In April 1906 Barker married Lillah McCarthy, an actress in his company, whom he had met some years earlier when they were both touring with Ben Greet. As Shaw had found in Barker a fascinating actor for his heroes, so he found in Miss McCarthy a delightful and skilled actress for his heroines. Both personally and professionally the marriage seemed a very successful match for almost ten years.

The success of the Court Theatre venture prompted the management to transfer for the 1907 – 1908 season to the larger, more attractive, and more fashionable Savoy Theatre in the Strand, where they repeated several of the Court productions and also did *The Devil's Disciple, Caesar and Cleopatra, Arms and the Man*, Gilbert Murray's *Medea*, and Galsworthy's *Joy*. After several other productions at various theaters, Barker managed a repertory season beginning on February 21, 1910, for Charles Frohman at the Duke of York's Theatre. This season was a commercial failure, although Galsworthy's *Justice* was a hit and Barker's own *The Madras House* met with some success. Next he and Lillah McCarthy in joint management presented a number of plays at the Little Theatre in John Street, Adelphi, the St. James's Theatre, and the Kingsway. Barker made his last appearance as an actor on the London stage in his translation of Schnitzler's *Anatol* at the Little Theatre in 1911. Then came Barker's most famous productions—Shakespeare's *The Winter's Tale* and *Twelfth Night* in 1912 and *A Midsummer Night's Dream* in 1914 at the Savoy.

In 1915 Barker brought his company to New York to appear in a repertory of plays consisting of Anatole France's *The Man Who Married a Dumb Wife* and Shaw's *Androcles and the Lion* on a double bill, Shakespeare's *A Midsummer Night's Dream* (which gave rise, as it had in London, to spirited comments about the gilded fairies), and Shaw's *The Doctor's Dilemma*. Barker showed his characteristic of doing the unusual also by presenting Greek tragedies in various football stadiums in America.

Barker's stay in America was of great importance in his personal life, for it was while he was in New York that he met and fell passionately in love with Helen Manchester Gates Huntington, an American novelist and poet. Lillah, long unwilling to accept the fact that he would not return to her, finally divorced Barker in April 1917, Mrs. Huntington divorced her husband in 1918, and she and Barker were married on July 31, 1918.

During the war Barker served first with the Red Cross in France, then as a cadet gunner, and finally as an intelligence officer in the British Army. He wrote little of consequence during this time: a small book called *The Red Cross in France;* an introduction to *One Man's View*, a novel by Leonard Merrick; and *Souls on Fifth*, a not very successful long short story.

After his marriage to Mrs. Huntington, the Barkers lived mainly in Devon until 1930, when they moved to Paris. Barker practically gave up his work as a producer, and he almost never saw Shaw again. According to Shaw, in the eyes of the second Mrs. Barker he was an undesirable acquaintance for her husband, and she had no sympathy with Socialism.[22] Barker did not, however, break his connections with the theater entirely. In 1919 he became the first chairman of the British Drama League, in which he was active for a dozen years. He produced his and his wife's translation of *The Romantic Young Lady* by

Martínez Sierra in 1920 and Maeterlinck's *The Betrothal* in 1921, and he took part in or supervised a few other productions. But his work as a producer was essentially finished.

Strangely enough, although earlier Barker had expressed the desire to devote more time to his writing, his original dramatic output after World War I was small. Only two full-length plays appeared between 1917 and his death—*The Secret Life* in 1923 and *His Majesty* in 1928, neither of which has been produced. He was not by any means idle, but he became interested in more scholarly pursuits. He continued to work for the advancement of drama by lecturing and writing on the importance of drama in society, on the need for a national theater, and on Shakespeare, in such works as *The Exemplary Theatre* (1924), *A National Theatre* (1930), and the *Prefaces to Shakespeare* (1923 – 1947). Much of his time was spent, too, on translations and adaptations of foreign plays, particularly the Spanish plays of Sierra and the Quinteros, on which Mrs. Barker collaborated.

Barker's prominence in the scholarly world as well as the theatrical may be seen in the fact that he received honorary doctor of letters degrees from Oxford and Reading universities and an honorary doctor of laws degree from Edinburgh, was a Fellow of the Royal Society of Literature, and served for two years beginning in 1937 as director of the British Institute of the University of Paris. During World War II he lectured in the United States at Harvard, Yale, and Princeton. Early in 1946 he returned to Paris, where he was working on a preface to *Macbeth* when he died on August 31, 1946.

Mrs. Barker lived in Paris until her death in February 1950. Lillah McCarthy married Sir Frederick Keeble, a noted botanist, in 1920, and virtually retired from the stage. She died on April 15, 1960.

Photographs of Barker at the age of thirty show a handsome face, with a strong jaw and firm mouth. His eyes were wide-set and his brows straight. He had straight hair and a clean-cut profile. A picture of about thirty years later reveals a face still handsome. The mouth is still firm and the hair still dark and abundant, though the forehead is high. But the expression in the eyes somehow seems sadder, and the brows rise toward the center of the forehead in a quizzical expression.

According to all reports, Barker's personality was strong and charming. Of all his friends, Shaw seems to have liked Barker the best. Hesketh Pearson reports that when he once asked Shaw which friend's company he had especially enjoyed, Shaw immediately named Granville Barker and only upon being prompted mentioned William Archer and Sidney Webb. Pearson concluded "that perhaps his happiest days were those when, with Granville-Barker acting the leading parts in his plays, he had first conquered the London stage at the Court Theatre. . . ."[23] Swinnerton says of Barker that "in his younger days he aroused the superstition of those who came under his spell, and some of them thought him inspired by God."[24] Even though published shortly after his death, when one would expect nothing but praise of him, the following account is well substantiated by others: "Actors who worked with him between 1919 and 1939 . . . soon found themselves at his feet. Those who had served him in earlier years never forgot their lost leader, and knew that without him their acting life would never be quite the same. And so it was with everyone who came within the sphere of his influence. They will always remember the exquisite form, and the eyes which could change so swiftly from the humorous to the quizzical, from the friendly to the stern. He inspired respect and affection wherever he went. A man of exalted spirit, and of no common clay."[25]

Barker's experience as an actor enabled him as a producer to understand the actor's problems and to show the actor, if necessary, what he wanted. His practical experience as actor and producer gave him an excellent foundation for playwriting. As a critic he could draw upon his personal knowledge of all of these areas, so that he spoke not just as a theoretician but as a practical man of the theater. As actor, producer, dramatist, and critic, Granville Barker had a profound influence on the English theater. His achievements in the first of these fields have been suggested in this chapter. His lasting contributions in the other three fields will be discussed in the chapters that follow.

Chapter Two
Producer, New Style

In the last decade of the nineteenth century the commercial theaters of England were presenting plays of little dramatic or literary merit, selected because of the opportunities they provided for the special ability or personality of the star, who often was an actor-manager controlling the production. The plays were constructed typically according to the "well-made" play formula which emphasized theatrical effect and careful plot development, making frequent use of inanimate objects (like the poisoned bouquet in *Adrienne Lecouvreur* by Scribe and Legouvé) and coincidence, and leading inevitably to the big scene, the *scène à faire*. Though the settings were often elaborately realistic, the plays were basically false in their melodramatic and sentimental presentation of life. Some writers, dramatists, and others interested in the well-being of the theater felt that the theater was capable of presenting a more truthful and more artistically valid view of life. These individuals wanted a chance for new dramatists to be heard; they wanted to break the bonds of commercialism in the theater. It is with this group associated with the "new" drama influenced by Ibsen that Granville Barker belongs as an actor, producer, and dramatist.

The beginning of the new movement may be said to have come with the founding of the Independent Theatre by J. T. Grein, critic of the *London Sunday Times*, and the performance of Ibsen's *Ghosts* on March 9, 1891. (*A Doll's House* had already been presented in London by Charles Charrington, who played Helmer, and Janet Achurch, who played Nora, in 1889.) The Independent Theatre in general followed the pattern of André Antoine's Théâtre Libre, founded in Paris in 1887, and Otto Brahm's Freie Bühne, founded in Berlin in 1889. Among the first members of this theatrical group were such distinguished writers as George Meredith, Thomas Hardy, George Moore, Arthur Wing Pinero, and Henry Arthur Jones. When the organization ended its activities in 1897, it had presented twenty-two productions, in which (including one-act plays) twenty-six new plays had been performed. One of them, in 1883, was *Widowers' Houses*, Shaw's first play.[1]

The next important step in the revival of English drama was the formation in 1899 of the Stage Society of London, which became the successor of the Independent Theatre. During thirteen seasons (to 1911) the Stage Society produced forty-six English plays and over twenty plays by continental dramatists—all but seven of them being produced for the first time in England. Among them were Shaw's *You Never Can Tell, Candida*, and *Captain Brassbound's Conversion*; Maeterlinck's *Interior* and *The Death of Tintagiles*; Hauptmann's *The Festival of Peace* and *Lonely Lives*; Ibsen's *The League of Youth* and *The Pillars of Society*; and Barker's *The Marrying of Ann Leete*. At first, performances were given privately on Sunday afternoons, in studios and whatever other suitable places could be found, then in theaters as the membership grew; then the Sunday performance was followed by another on Monday afternoon. Incorporated in 1904, the Society operated on a subscription basis, paying its own way.[2] It made significant contributions in the discovery of new actors and producers, the introduction to England of important foreign plays in translation, and the opportunity it gave for new English playwrights to be heard.

One of the new theatrical personages that the Stage Society brought to the fore was Granville Barker. As an actor he had already attracted attention. As a member of the Stage Society he continued to act; he moved into producing as well (he produced Maeterlinck's *Interior* and *The Death of Tintagiles* and Fiona MacLeod's *The House of Usna*); and he emerged as a promising new playwright when the Society in 1902 presented his first play written alone, *The Marrying of Ann Leete*, with Barker himself as producer.

Although Barker did some work as a producer for the Stage Society, his first important contributions in this field came during the Vedrenne-Barker management of the Court Theatre from October 18, 1904, to June 29, 1907, which has been widely recognized as a most important period in English stage history. Hesketh Pearson, for example, calls it "the most shining event in the story of our drama since the time of Shakespeare."[3] In 1904, when J. H. Leigh was giving a series of Shakespeare revivals at the Court with J. E. Vedrenne as his manager, Barker was asked to take charge of the production of *The Two Gentlemen of Verona.* He agreed, with the stipulation that Vedrenne join him in giving six matinee performances of *Candida.*[4] Both productions were very successful. Out of this arrangement grew the alliance between the two men, with Vedrenne as business manager and Barker as artistic director, which lasted for several years and which resulted in bringing to the attention of the English public a number of British dramatists (including Shaw, Galsworthy, and Barker himself) as well as continental playwrights. After the success of the *Candida* matinees, others of Shaw's plays were done with Barker in the leading roles, and Shaw, according to his own account, "became playwright in ordinary to this new enterprise."[5]

Shaw was indeed the dramatist whose work was most often presented at the Court. Thirty-two plays by seventeen authors were given for a total of 988 performances; of these, 701 were performances of eleven plays by Shaw—*Man and Superman* (176 performances), *You Never Can Tell* (149), *John Bull's Other Island* (121), *Captain Brassbound's Conversion* (89), *Major Barbara* (52), *The Doctor's Dilemma* (50), *Candida* (33), *How He Lied to Her Husband* (9), *The Philanderer* (8), *Don Juan in Hell* and *The Man of Destiny* (double bill, 8). Although the Stage Society had presented some Shaw, and although he had been successfully presented in Germany and in New York, the English commercial theaters were not interested in his unorthodox plays.[6] It remained for the Court Theatre to become a showcase for Shaw. Without Shaw's plays (which he produced himself) the Court venture might well have not been so successful, but the reverse is also true. When asked: Do you credit the Court with affording your plays production when they might otherwise not have achieved it at the time, Shaw understandably replied, "Nonsense! I should have achived [*sic*] my position somehow."[7] Yet the fact remains that Shaw's reputation as a dramatist was established by the Court Theatre productions.

One of the disadvantages of the commercial theater, in Barker's view, was the long-run system, because it limited the number of plays that could be done and because it had a deadening effect on the actors. At the Court no play was presented for more than a few weeks at a time, and usually in modified repertory with another, often with one being done in the evenings and the other in the afternoons.

Although there was a preponderance of Shaw in the total number of performances, a great many other authors were represented, both English and continental, classical and modern. Next to Shaw, the most popular was Barker himself. *Prunella* (by Barker and Laurence Housman) was given forty-eight times and *The Voysey Inheritance* thirty-four. Euripides was third, with *Electra* and *Hippolytus* each given twenty times and *The Trojan Women* eight. Galsworthy's *The Silver Box* had a total of twenty-nine performances. Others represented were Elizabeth Robins, St. John Hankin, William Butler Yeats, Cyril Harcourt, John Masefield, Maurice Hewlett, Robert Vernon Harcourt, Frederick Fenn, Hauptmann, Schnitzler, Ibsen, and Maeterlinck.[8] One of the accomplishments of the Court Theatre under the Vedrenne-Barker management, then, was to enable new dramatists to be heard in England. The wide variety of authors, attitudes, and types of plays presented indicates, as MacCarthy points out, the remarkably wide sympathies of the managers. The only criterion was quality. Significantly, however, many of the plays were not conventional in their construction. The Court productions, as MacCarthy says, broadened the idea of what a play could be, expanded the concept of the term "dramatic"; they helped to change the emphasis in drama from external to internal action, from plot to characterization and the emotional and moral content of the situation.[9]

As a producer Barker was very exacting. The fine results he achieved were undoubtedly due not only to his insight and experience but also to hard work with his actors. He demanded such long hours of rehearsal that Shaw says he warned him that the result would be laws limiting hours of rehearsal the way working hours in a factory were limited.[10] Barker insisted that the actor in order to interpret faithfully the life of his time must mingle familiarly in it.[11] This belief in a close tie between art and society is evident in Barker's own work as a dramatist, too, and in his faith that the theater can and should be a great moral and educational force in national life. He believed that each actor should see the character he was portraying as part of the whole, and so each person had a copy of the entire play for rehearsals rather than simply pages with his own lines and cues.[12] Moreover,

Barker believed that the actor should possess an intimate knowledge of the character he was portraying, not just recite the lines written for him by the dramatist; that the actor should think about the influences in the character's past which made him what he was. The lengthy stage directions he provides in his own plays are an illustration of this sort of biographical and psychological interest in his characters. In producing a play he would tell the actors the entire history of the characters and suggest the influence on their personalities of things in that history and in their environment. He once said to an actor: "You are not, I hope, going to tell me that the man drops from the skies, ready-made, at the moment you make your first entrance."[13]

The acting at the Court achieved a new degree of realism. The impression it created, according to one contemporary writer, was of a complete lack of artificiality. Instead of the slow and emphatic underlining of every point and exaggeration of every sentiment that were characteristic of the old style of acting, Barker stressed quickness. The actor must have quickness of voice, fluency of gesture, and alertness of intellect, "which can pass easily from thought to thought, from emotion to emotion, which understands the art of hinting and taking things for granted, and knows how to be expressive by skill rather than by force."[14]

At the Court a new high was reached in excellence in acting, not in the sense of virtuoso individual performances, but in unity and totality of effect. Borsa, for example, says: ". . . The acting is perfect. There are no stars (blessed relief!), but the company always numbers excellent actors and actresses among its members. Mr Granville Barker . . . devotes such care to the welding together of the different elements that the result is invariably a happy and harmonious whole. In the matter of ensemble the performances at the Court stand on a level with that which ruled once on a time at Antoine's Théâtre Libre."[15] Whitworth says that there was a "spiritual realism" in the acting at the Court, with Barker drawing out the best in each actor, using his own skill as an actor to demonstrate when necessary, and following his belief as a playwright that the author's intention is of paramount importance.[16] Pearson calls Barker "the greatest producer of his time in England" and says he revolutionized stage production by emphasizing detail and team work.[17]

Among the names of actors in the programs of the Court Theatre during these three years are a number that were already famous or became so later—Walter Hampden, Edmund Gwenn, Ellen Terry, Dion Boucicault, Aubrey Smith, and Mrs. Patrick Campbell. Distinguished actors these, but no one was allowed to outshine the others in a production, not even Mrs. Campbell. Mrs. Campbell appeared in *Hedda Gabler* in a series of seven matinees during three weeks in 1906. According to MacCarthy, her performance was perfect, but so was the entire play remarkably acted. "It speaks wonders for the Court Theatre management," says he, "that she did not act the others off the stage."[18] Mrs. Campbell was extremely disappointed that despite the success of *Hedda* Barker refused to let it go on for an extended run. She had spent more on her wardrobe than the salary she received and had looked forward to a run of months. She did all she could to persuade Barker, but he was adamant. Her contract was only for seven matinees, after which the play was taken off the Court boards, although Mrs. Campbell did, with Barker's permission, take this translation of the play to the provinces and to America.[19]

As Barker the actor impressed the critics with his charm, so Barker the producer similarly affected his co-workers. Walter Hampden, for example, who appeared early in his career in a small part in *Aglavaine and Selysette* at the Court, remembered him as pleasant and attractive.[20] But along with his attractiveness, Barker apparently had strong determination and something of a temper. Shaw states that at the Court Barker "liked to have his own way."[21] Pearson says that Barker could become annoyed and show his annoyance by a terrifying look at the offending person and a turning of his back or the doing of a few dance steps.[22] Usually, however, according to Pearson, Barker was quiet and friendly in his manner and gained the actor's complete cooperation by treating him as a brother and by inspiring him with self-confidence.[23] Nor did Barker lose interest once a play had been rehearsed and presented. He would watch a performance occasionally and send notes to members of the cast with messages like "You are acting. Why?" or "You are not acting. Why not?" or "How serious you are getting!" or "Remember this is a comedy."[24]

Not all of the plays at the Court were equally well done, but the standards were remarkably high. Shaw, who produced his own plays

at the Court, maintains that Barker was not always at his best with
Shaw and Shakespeare. According to him, "Barker's production of his
own plays and Galsworthy's was exquisite [because] their styles were
perfectly sympathetic, whereas his style and taste were as different
from mine as Debussy's from Verdi's."[25] Says Shaw: "He had never
seen great acting and hated it, whereas I, having seen it in my
boyhood and been stagestruck by it, always wrote for it. He used to
say to the company when I was rehearsing, 'Remember, will you, that
this is Italian opera.' His own style was lowtoned, and even in his
Shakespear [*sic*] productions the big parts were underplayed."[26]

The Greek tragedies presented at the Court were apparently not
completely successful. According to MacCarthy, they were not done
in archaic style, nor was music introduced to increase the effect on the
audience's emotions, but rather they were acted as if they had been
written for the modern stage, except for the chorus, which is perforce
an artificial device. MacCarthy describes the chorus as being a failure.
". . . It was represented by seven or eight ladies, who moved about
with slow, elaborate caution, posed like *tableaux vivants*, and uttered
the most various sentiments in a monotonous and lugubrious chant,
tapering into dismal contralto notes, and conveying no definite
emotion, beyond suggesting the earnest desire of the performers
themselves to do their best."[27] At any rate, however, the productions
were successful enough to encourage Gilbert Murray to continue to
translate all of Euripides' extant plays and thus gain a reputation as
the leading expert in his own day in Greek drama.[28]

It was in productions of contemporary drama that the Court
excelled. An outstanding example of realism in overall effect was the
representation of a crowd at a suffragist meeting in Trafalgar Square in
the second act of Elizabeth Robins's *Votes for Women*. Attending a
performance of this play, Otto Kahn was so impressed, according to a
contemporary American magazine account, that by the second act he
had decided that Barker was the man to be director of the "millionaires' theater" which he and a group of other wealthy men were
planning for New York City. He made Barker an offer "such as was
never made to a manager since the world began. At the end of a few
years he could retire and live on his income while devoting his leisure
to play writing." The anonymous writer concludes by insisting that

Barker "must come, for his coming will mean everything to dramatic art in America."[29] Barker was interested enough to go to America in 1908 while considering this offer, but he decided against accepting it because the theater that was being built would be too large for the successful presentation of the kind of intellectual drama with which he was primarily concerned.

The Court Theatre venture, with its new plays of intellectual content, its new, less flamboyant, more natural style of acting emphasizing teamwork rather than the special abilities of a star, and its concern with an overall truthful presentation of life, had succeeded in attracting the attention of enough of the British public to make the producers ambitious for something more. The audiences, to be sure, were composed not of the wide general public but rather of the intelligentsia—persons of culture and students, with a mixture of society people.[30] They came in sufficient numbers, however, to encourage a transfer by the management of the Court for the 1907–1908 season to a larger and more centrally located theater, the Savoy, seating 1,070 as compared with the Court's 670. Artistically the success of the Court was continued at the Savoy, though financially the venture was a failure. Several of the earlier productions were repeated, and others added—Shaw's *The Devil's Disciple, Caesar and Cleopatra, Arms and the Man;* Gilbert Murray's translation of Euripides' *Medea*, and Galsworthy's *Joy*. Barker's *Waste* was to have been done, but it was banned by the censor because of references to an abortion.[31] The Vedrenne-Barker management also presented Shaw's *Getting Married* and Masefield's *The Tragedy of Nan* at the Haymarket Theatre,[32] and in March 1909 Barker produced Galsworthy's *Strife* in a series of matinees at the Duke of York's Theatre for Charles Frohman.[33]

Then, beginning on February 21, 1910, Barker served as the chief producer during a seventeen-week repertory season at the Duke of York's for Charles Frohman. Barker's successful experience at the Court is credited with being the inspiration not only for Frohman's Repertory Theatre at the Duke of York's, but also for three others— A. E. F. Horniman's Manchester Repertory Theatre (established in 1907), the first repertory theater in Great Britain; the Scottish Repertory Theatre, at the Royalty in Glasgow, opened in April 1909;

and the New Theatre in New York, opened on November 8, 1909.[34]

The Repertory Theatre at the Duke of York's was not a success financially, though among the works done were Galsworthy's *Justice*, Shaw's *Misalliance*, Meredith's *The Sentimentalists*, Barrie's *The Twelve-Pound Look*, Pinero's *Trelawney of the "Wells,"* Housman and Barker's *Prunella*, and Barker's *The Madras House*. Shaw produced his own play, Dion Boucicault did the Barrie and Pinero plays, and Barker produced the rest.[35] Artistically the standards established at the Court were continued. The acting was similarly naturalistic, as was the overall staging. Various suggestions have been made to explain the financial failure of this repertory season: the critics labeled each of the successive productions as "not a play" because it was not a play in the old "well-made" play formula;[36] the public thought the plays somber, though they included comedy and fantasy; there was perhaps confusion in the direction as Barker was gradually deprived of complete independence; the expenses were greater because of increased advertising and the costs of operating a larger theater (1,094 seats).[37] Nevertheless the season is important in the history of repertory theater, and Barker's reputation as a producer of modern plays, already established at the Court, was enhanced.

After the repertory season at the Duke of York's, Barker produced *The Witch* by Masefield at the Court and his own translation of Schnitzler's *The Farewell Supper* at the Palace before he and Lillah McCarthy went into joint management in 1911 at the Little Theatre. There Barker's translation of Schnitzler's *Anatol* was done, followed by Ibsen's *The Master Builder*, Shaw's *Fanny's First Play*, and Barker's one-act play *Rococo* on a triple bill with Meredith's *The Sentimentalists* and Barrie's *The Twelve-Pound Look*. *Fanny's First Play* was a long-run hit, being transferred at the beginning of 1912 to the Kingsway, where Barker went on to produce Phillpotts's *The Secret Woman* and Gilbert Murray's translation of Euripides' *Iphigenia in Taurus*.[38]

The next step in Barker's career brought him lasting fame as a producer of Shakespeare. His reputation in this field is based on three productions at the Savoy under his joint management with Lillah McCarthy: *The Winter's Tale* and *Twelfth Night* in 1912 and *A Midsummer Night's Dream* in 1914. These productions are landmarks in the history of Shakespeare on the stage. Just as Shaw and Barker had been a notable combination at the Court, so were Shakespeare and Barker at the Savoy. Barker's productions were outstanding in their differences from what had become the traditional way of doing Shakespeare. They were increasingly popular with audiences and received much attention from the critics of the day for their fidelity to Shakespeare's text and for the "decoration," about the success of which there were strong differences of opinion.

During the eighteenth and nineteenth centuries Shakespeare's plays had quite generally been presented with many cuts, interpolations, and rearrangements of lines and scenes. These changes were necessitated largely by the long waits for the shifting of the extremely elaborate, heavy, realistic scenery that had become traditional with the great actor-managers. Charles Kean, for example, in his productions at the Princess Theatre from 1851 to 1859, emphasized spectacle in scenery and costumes based on archeological and historical studies to such an extent that George Macready in 1860 described Kean's productions as "scenes annotated by text." Irving's productions, less elaborate than Kean's, still freely cut and rearranged the text. Beerbohm Tree's productions at His Majesty's between 1898 and 1911 varied in their physical spectacle, but at their most elaborate they cut one third of the text. [39] The blank verse was spoken in a slow, elocutionary manner, according to a contemporary reviewer, that "disregards so completely not only the sense but the feeling expressed in the lines, that an audience can scarcely be cajoled into listening for more than a few minutes at a time." So the producer "crowds the stage with elaborate scenery and clothes, he hires an orchestra to play slow music during the longer speeches, and every few minutes he arranges a piece of ingenious 'business' to distract the audience from the *longueurs* of the words. . . ."[40]

There were some producers who believed in simpler productions and more of Shakespeare's text. The most important of these was William Poel, whose ideas about producing Shakespeare Barker had come into contact with early in his career, having appeared as Richard II in one of Poel's presentations. Poel attempted to return to the Elizabethan style of staging with a complete lack of scenery. Barker did not go this far by any means, but he did, with simple settings, eliminate the long pauses for shifting scenery, and he had the actors

speak the lines quickly, thus managing to give more of the text as
Shakespeare wrote it.

In an interview in New York City in 1915 in connection with his
presentation there of several plays (including *A Midsummer Night's
Dream*), Barker explained his ideas about Shakespearean production.
He believed in giving the play as Shakespeare wrote it, without
cutting or adding anything, although he did allow for certain excep-
tions, because "to retain obscenities and jokes that are not understood
by modern audiences is as foolish as to cut too much. It is perfectly
possible to give the gems of the plays but it is not possible to set them
in subordinate scenes of shadow or swift action, as Shakespeare wrote
them, if the text is ruthlessly cut. Either he knew how to write plays
or he didn't."

What Barker advocated instead of elaborate scenery was a method
of staging which he called "decoration." He explained that he was
"for realism as much as anyone else, but you can't do Shakespeare
realistically." His productions made use not of painted scenery but of
curtains (sometimes decorated with formal designs), pillars, cone-
shaped cutouts for trees, and colorful costumes. Although Barker
himself did not design the costumes or the settings, still the final
credit (or blame) went, and should go, to him. The presentations
showed the influence of the Gordon Craig and Max Reinhardt ideas of
staging in that much use was made of color and line and lighting—
not in an attempt to simulate reality but to suggest atmosphere. The
stage was reconstructed to have three playing levels: the portion
behind the proscenium arch, the floor raised, with a couple of steps
leading up to it; a middle area under and in front of the proscenium
arch, which had a false proscenium within it, making it smaller; and
an apron built out over the orchestra pit at a lower level, extending to
the stage boxes, which became entrances to this front stage area.
Instead of footlights, spotlights were placed in front of the balcony.[41]

The production of *A Winter's Tale* at the Savoy on September 21,
1912, called forth a mixed response to just about every aspect of it.
Where one critic praised the settings by Norman Wilkinson (a gold
curtain with white pilasters, for example, to suggest a palace),[42]
another disliked the "decoration."[43] The costumes by Albert Rothenstein (later Rutherston) were admitted by one critic to be beautiful if

calling too much attention to themselves,[44] whereas another made sarcastic comments about their resemblances to the Russian ballet and the Chelsea Club Ball and their comically bizarre effect.[45] Critics liked the arrangement of the three levels of the stage and the faithfulness to the text; they were unhappy with the speed with which the lines were spoken and the lack of feeling for the poetry. The *Times* reviewer, after making fun of the costumes, concluded by saying: "It is all very startling and provocative and audacious, and on the whole we like it."[46] John Palmer judged that this was "probably the first performance of a play by Shakespeare that the author would himself have recognized for his own since Burbage—or, at any rate, Davenant—retired from active management."[47] Darrell Figgis in his review made an accurate prediction: "Nevertheless, despite the fact that the hand of the artist made impertinent intrusions on the proper business of the dramatist, the production was an excellent one, and, in the courage of some of its departures, we venture to say that it will be a memorable one."[48]

Although *A Winter's Tale* ran for only six weeks and lost money, *Twelfth Night* ran from November 15, 1912, to March 13, 1913, and was more generally acclaimed by the critics. The method of staging was the same as with *The Winter's Tale*, with Norman Wilkinson this time designing both settings and costumes, which perhaps created a more unified effect. The *Illustrated London News* called the production "a triumph by virtue of its adoption of more conciliatory methods" than were used in the earlier work, and went on to say that "the poetry and sense of the lines are not in this case sacrificed in the aim at speed. . . . We are taught afresh by Mr Barker that romance need not be dull, that the poetic drama need not be overloaded with spectacle."[49] Darrell Figgis in *Academy* did not like the "picturesque" costumes or the pink and white settings or the "doll's house-y" cutout trees, but he praised the "beauty and rhythm" of the lines, spoken "swiftly and with a rhythmic cadence."[50] Harold Child in the *Times* liked the physical beauty of the production and the tempo and found it "great fun."[51] John Palmer in the *Saturday Review* said: "It lives. The dead weight of silly tradition . . . has dropped away. . . . Mr. Barker's company in 'Twelfth Night,' as in 'A Winter's Tale,' bring us more nearly in touch with the spirit of their author than any yet seen in modern London."[52] In his Shakespearean productions as in his earlier modern ones, Barker allowed no star to dominate the play but rather strove for teamwork and unity of effect. That he succeeded in *Twelfth Night* is seen from this comment by John Drinkwater: "Looking back some years I can recall two productions of 'Twelfth Night,' one by Sir Herbert Tree and one by Mr. Granville-Barker, and in the one case I remember nothing but a very vivid performance of Malvolio, while of the other I retain an exact impression of a great comedy beautifully balanced and artistically complete."[53]

On February 6, 1914, Barker presented a third major Shakespearean effort at the Savoy, *A Midsummer Night's Dream*, in a production which caused more violent reaction than either of the earlier ones, but which ran to May 9. Norman Wilkinson was again the designer not only of the sets but of the costumes as well. Although this time the entire production was more colorful, the thing that really caused a sensation was the gilded fairies. They were completely gold—covered from head to foot in gold costumes and gold paint, including their faces. Puck, in contrast, was in scarlet with a rough wig and baggy pants. The *Academy* reviewer disliked the fairies, calling them "bronze-green imps from an outrageous nightmare."[54] On the other hand, the *Athenaeum* critic said, "The first scene in which the fairy nation appears is a triumphant spectacle, nor can it be denied that by this device they are admirably separated from the human inhabitants of the play."[55] J. E. Harold Terry in the *British Review* thought the fairies "an inspiration" but too "obviously of Eastern origin" instead of English.[56] Unquestionably no commentator could ignore the fairies. In this production as in the earlier ones the text was uncut, the lines were spoken quickly, there was only one intermission, and stage business that had become conventional was left out.

Striking and untraditional as these productions were, did they have any effect on later revivals of Shakespeare? Indications are that they definitely did. During World War I and after, Barker's influence was quite apparent. His methods were followed at the Old Vic, by Barry Jackson at the Birmingham Repertory (which gave seventeen of Shakespeare's plays between 1914 and 1923), and by the New Shakespeare Company at Stratford under W. Bridges-Adams. They all used simple settings and quick speech, and emphasized continuous action, complete texts, and teamwork.[57] Tyrone Guthrie acknowledges his indebtedness to Barker in his Shakespeare productions in the elimination of realistic scenery and the use of a permanent "structure," with the actors close to the audience, with no cuts and no pauses for scene changes.[58] M. St. Clare Byrne, in evaluating the condition of Shakespeare production in the middle of the twentieth century, points out the emphasis on presenting the full text and acceptance of the "idea that the author knew his business." Byrne credits Poel and Barker with showing the importance of understanding Shakespeare's dramatic technique as an aid to understanding the content of the play, of requiring from the scenic designer a setting which, using the resources of the modern stage, provides the characteristics of the Elizabethan theater, and of establishing the producer as the one in charge of a unified interpretation of the dramatist's intent.[59] Although Barker's ideas and methods have not been followed completely in the years after his revolutionary productions, their influence has most definitely been felt.

After the first two Shakespeare productions, the Barkers presented (in the fall of 1913) Shaw's *Androcles and the Lion* at the St. James's on a double bill with *The Harlequinade*, which Barker wrote with Dion Clayton Calthrop, followed by a three-week repertory season.[60] After *A Midsummer Night's Dream*, Barker produced his own arrangement of parts of Hardy's *The Dynasts*, which ran from November 14, 1914, to January 7, 1915.[61]

Early in 1915 under the auspices of the New York Stage Society, Barker presented a company, including Lillah McCarthy, in a repertory of plays in New York City. David Belasco was then the greatest producer in the country, and since Barker's methods were in contrast to Belasco's realism in settings, comparisons were naturally made. Barker did not like the sort of publicity which made him out to be a trailblazer and a corrector of the faults of other workers in the theater. Certainly this sort of attitude on his part—even though others might only have fancied that it existed—would not have endeared him to Belasco and other American producers, and Barker was wise enough to realize it. In an interview in New York he is quoted thus: "Mr. Granville Barker wishes to have it understood that he is not a prophet and is not here to save anybody's soul. . . . He is not an uprooter or upbuilder. He has been trying to say this for a long time, but nobody will listen to him. He chooses a play to present and then sets his style for it out of any ideas that seem to be applicable. If he were to present a Belasco play, he would probably give it a Belasco setting."[62] It was, moreover, pointed out by several contemporary commentators that Belasco had already used the "innovations" that Barker was credited with having introduced. In a production of the Passion Play in California he extended the stage and eliminated footlights; in Sophocles' *Electra* in New York and Boston in 1899 he used the apron stage and extreme simplification of scenic detail; in *The Darling of the Gods* and *Peter Grimm* he extended the stage over a portion of the orchestra seats.[63] A speaker at a Drama League meeting called it Barker's greatest triumph in New York when Belasco produced *Marie-Odile* without footlights, said Louis V. De Foe in the *New York World*. But De Foe pointed out: "All who have a definite knowledge of the theater know that Mr. Belasco's stage is constructed for the omission of footlights when the artistic needs of his productions demand other methods of lighting, and that, while it is not provided with an 'apron,' it is equipped with an extension which serves much the same purpose." Thus did New York defend its own against the suggestion that Barker's productions were the inspiration for Belasco's methods. Moreover, De Foe said that Barker recognized the injustice of such suggestions "by his uncomfortable wincing when the ill-considered reflection against the leading dramatic producer in this country was being made."[64]

Contemporary articles like these are good evidence of the fact that Barker made a great stir in America's theatrical capital. His coming was hailed in the title of one article as "The Stage Event of the Year,"[65] and there were many articles about his new methods of staging. Barker presented four plays in New York: Anatole France's *The Man Who Married a Dumb Wife* and Shaw's *Androcles and the Lion* on a double bill, Shakespeare's *A Midsummer Night's Dream*, and Shaw's *The Doctor's Dilemma*.

The first of these productions was designed by the American Robert Edmond Jones. It was highly praised by one writer as a "joy," and "sophisticated modernism of the most tactful and imaginative kind." The contrast to Belasco's realism was noted: "Where Mr.

Belasco would put in the skin, the seeds, the indigestible and innutritious trash, under the illusion that if anything is real orange it must be palatable, Mr. Jones has given us only golden fruit, assimilable, ripe."[66] Another writer called it a "merry and beautiful production, . . . set upon the stage with extraordinary charm and effectiveness, and acted with a perfection of ensemble that was a continual delight." Here was the new stagecraft, with "the sense of a vigorous and poetically imaginative intelligence pervading, ordering, and unifying the whole."[67]

Androcles and the Lion was praised quite as much as *The Dumb Wife*. According to one critic, it saved Barker's work "from the clutches of the faddists and poseurs, the *précieux*, the pseudo-intellectuals" because it was such good fun even for the lowbrows.[68] It was called by another a "superb production" with a "remarkable cast," including O. P. Heggie as Androcles and Lillah McCarthy as Lavinia.[69] The play itself was praised, as were Albert Rothenstein's settings. And everything was given "just the right balance by the nimble Mr. Barker."[70] *The Doctor's Dilemma*, the last of the plays done in New York, was also commended for its acting and setting.[71]

About *A Midsummer Night's Dream* the New York critics felt much as had the London reviewers. It was the gilded fairies again that especially aroused comment and disagreement. Gilman quotes Barker's statement about the fairies in his preface to the play: "How should they look? I realize that when there is perhaps no really right thing to do one is always tempted to do too much. . . . They must not be too startling. . . . I won't have them dowdy. They musn't warp your imagination—stepping too boldly between Shakespeare's spirit and yours." Yet this, Gilman feels, is exactly what the fairies did—they called attention to themselves. But he compliments the production by saying that it seldom was boring, although productions of this play usually are. He praises the rapid performance, at the same time lamenting the loss of poetic beauty in the delivery of the lines. His conclusion is: "Yet perhaps, if we are to have the 'Dream' upon the stage at all, this is the best way in which to present it there."[72] Francis Hackett felt that the production and especially the fairies lacked "the charm of the elfin wood." Although he granted it "a great deal of charm as a spectacle," he concluded: "It cannot be acclaimed as a perfect marriage between the dramatist and his producer. It is only a picturesque flirtation."[73] Norman Hapgood stated that the production "has given intense delight to many exceptionally intelligent persons who appreciate decorative art and its relation to the stage," and recognized Barker as a master in that field. His conclusion is that "it is enough merely to rejoice that an eternal masterpiece has appeared in its entirety, with lovely music and dances and pictures, on the New York stage, and emerges from the ordeal with the triumph of having at least stimulated keen and serious discussion of questions connected with stage art and poetic drama."[74] The production was not an unqualified success, then, but it did serve in New York as in London as a fine example of the new decorative method of staging Shakespeare, a method which allowed closer fidelity to the original play because of the elimination of elaborate realistic scenery, and it, along with his other productions, served to substantiate in the New World the reputation which Barker had achieved as a producer in England.

After these productions at Wallack's Theatre in New York, Barker in the spring of 1915 presented a series of performances of Greek tragedies (Euripides' *The Trojan Women* and *Iphigenia in Taurus*, both translated by Gilbert Murray) in college football stadiums. These productions came about more as a result of chance and inspiration than of lengthy consideration. On a trip to New Haven during the winter, Barker visited the new Yale Bowl and at once commented on its possibilities for the performance of a Greek tragedy. This turned out to be not simply an idle remark, for he followed it up. A committee including Professor George Baker of Harvard and Professor William Lyon Phelps of Yale helped make Barker's plan a reality, with the result being a series of eleven afternoon performances in five college stadiums, beginning at Yale on May 15 with *Iphigenia*, going to Harvard for both *Iphigenia* and *The Trojan Women*, then to the University of Pennsylvania for both, then to the College of the City of New York for four performances, and closing on June 11 and 12 at Princeton. Norman Wilkinson was the designer for the productions. In *Iphigenia* striking color effects were created—the chorus being costumed in black and orange and the soldiers in black and white with red plumes. In *The Trojan Women* the colors were more somber—

black, grey, and purple. The stage was a platform one hundred feet wide with equally wide steps leading up to it and with three doors in a back wall forty feet high, suggesting the area in front of a temple. The location of this stage in the stadium would determine the size of the amphitheater formed. Barker's was not the first presentation of Greek drama in an outdoor amphitheater in America, but it was the first on such a large scale.[75] These productions were well received, and they served to demonstrate Barker's willingness to experiment as a producer.

This season in America was virtually the end of Barker's career as a producer. The war interrupted his work, and after his second marriage he did not resume full-time activities in the theater. He did produce, in 1920, *The Romantic Young Lady* by Martínez Sierra in a translation by himself and the second Mrs. Barker and, in 1921, Maeterlinck's *The Betrothal*, which was the last production for which he was entirely responsible. He participated in the production of his version of Guitry's *Deburau* in 1921 and of his and his wife's translation of Sierra's *The Kingdom of God* in 1927; he supervised productions of *The Voysey Inheritance* in 1934 and of *Waste* in 1936; and he worked with Lewis Casson in a production of *King Lear* at the Old Vic in 1940 with John Gielgud in the title role.

Although he was no longer regularly or fully involved in producing, he did not, however, lose any of his ability. John Gielgud describes an experience with Barker during rehearsals of *Fortunato* and *The Lady from Alfaqueque*, two plays by Serafín and Joaquín Álvarez Quintero, translated by Barker and his second wife, which were being presented at the Court Theatre in 1928. One morning the Barkers came to the rehearsal. The actors were extremely nervous when Barker appeared. Gielgud's account of what followed well illustrates Barker's ability and the fact that he impressed Gielgud as someone almost superhuman and godlike:

Barker was certainly a revelation. He rehearsed us for about two hours, changed nearly every move and arrangement of the stage, acted, criticised, advised, in an easy flow of practical efficiency, never stopping for a moment. We all sat spellbound, trying to drink in his words of wisdom and at the same time to remember all the hints he was giving us, none of which we had time to write down or memorise. Everything he said was obviously and irrefutably right. . . . Finally we came to my last and best scene. . . .

Barker showed me exactly how to play this scene—the business, the timing, everything which would make it effective in performance. I implored him to wait a moment and let me rehearse it two or three times running, but he looked at his watch, signed to Mrs. Barker, who was concealed somewhere in the dress-circle, bade us all good-morning, and disappeared through the front of the house, never to return.[76]

Thus, although Barker returned only on rare occasions to active work in the theater after the war, the skill which he exhibited on those occasions indicated that his reputation as a producer was well founded.

Barker's main activities and areas of influence as a producer may be divided into two parts—the production of modern plays and the production of Shakespeare, and his characteristic style of production may be divided into the naturalistic and the more imaginative and suggestive. In the modern plays his method was naturalistic, whereas in the Shakespearean productions, particularly in the "decoration," his aim was not at all to reproduce actual life, although there was an emphasis on naturalness in acting and in speech even in these productions (sometimes, at least, to the detriment of the poetic beauty of the lines). In his work as a dramatist, too, there is evident a combination of naturalism and romanticism.

Barker's contributions to the English drama in his work as a producer are many. He was the chief influence in the early twentieth century in England toward a naturalistic style of acting and production. He did much to advance the repertory idea, with emphasis on ensemble performance rather than on concentration on star virtuosity. He helped greatly to popularize the plays of Shaw and introduced to English audiences a number of other new authors, both English and continental, who proved to be important. His productions drew back to the theater many intelligent playgoers who had become weary of the old-fashioned melodramas and well-made plays. His Shakespearean productions influenced later producers to abandon elaborate attempts at cumbersome realistic scenery and restored the original Shakespeare to the stage without cuts, interpolations, and rearrangements. He did much to put into practice the Gordon Craig theory of the drama as the unified combination of all the arts. Barker, in fact, made the producer (as distinct from the actor-manager) an important figure in the theater and raised him to the level of being an artist. As this kind of producer he became one of the outstanding theatrical figures of his day and of the entire history of the English theater.

Yet, as the work of the actor is ephemeral, so, too, is the work of the theatrical producer. In his own plays and in his criticism Barker made more permanent contributions to the English theater. Indeed his *Prefaces to Shakespeare* are in a sense productions of the plays within the covers of a book. In his days of active work in the theater Barker's fame as a producer outshone his reputation as a dramatist. Shaw, for one, however, believed that too much attention had been paid to Barker the producer and not enough by far to Barker the author.[77] His plays are certainly worthy of study. The following chapters present discussions in chronological order of each of his published plays, followed by a general description and evaluation of Barker the dramatist.

Chapter Three

Two Rebellious Heroines: *The Marrying of Ann Leete* and *Prunella*

The Marrying of Ann Leete

Robert Browning once wrote: "I never designedly tried to puzzle people, as some of my critics supposed. On the other hand, I never pretended to offer such literature as should be a substitute for a cigar or a game at dominoes to an idle man." The first of the plays that Granville Barker wrote by himself, *The Marrying of Ann Leete* (written in 1899; produced on January 26, 1902), assuredly is not satisfying in the way a cigar is after a hearty meal; seeing it or reading it is not a pleasant way to relax after a tiring day at the office. It is not the sort of play a salesman would take his best customer to for an evening's entertainment, nor is it the sort of play women would flock to on Wednesday matinees. Even a man as experienced in the theater as William Archer complained that it was difficult to understand.[1] But then it was not produced in the commercial theater for audiences seeking light diversion. It was one of many avant-garde plays of the day to be presented by the Stage Society of London. These plays, including some by Ibsen and Shaw, were almost all dramas of thought and purpose, and dramas that remain important in dramatic literature. So Barker's play was in distinguished company, presented to an audience not averse to some intellectual effort on its part.

Before Shaw's *Man and Superman*, published and produced in 1903, *The Marrying of Ann Leete* presents the idea of the Life Force (though Barker does not call it that) bringing about the mating of two individuals whom their associates would not expect to see wed. The play is primarily the study of a family, a subject with which Barker deals in later plays, too. The head of the family is Carnaby Leete, an unscrupulous, practical, cynical, brilliant politician who has changed sides in politics once before to his personal advantage and is about to do so again. He has married off one of his daughters, Sarah, for his political gain, and wants to do the same with the young Ann. The wording of the title is significant—it is the "marrying" of Ann Leete, not simply her marriage, which is the material of the play. Leete would have her married to Lord John Carp, a man twice her age, but Ann suddenly proposes to John Abud, a young, healthy gardener, and marries him instead. To guide her in her choice she has the experience of Sarah, whose loveless match has caused her only misery, and of her brother George, who has married (for love) the daughter of Farmer Crowe, who ironically has once rejected Abud as a candidate for his daughter's hand because he wants his daughter's husband to be of a higher social position.

Although written when Barker was but twenty-two, the play in many ways shows great originality and skill in technique. The curtain rises on a quiet, dark stage—it is the Leete garden at four o'clock in the morning. Suddenly a woman's scream breaks the stillness. Then we hear Lord John Carp apologize to Ann for having kissed her. Gradually the sky lightens with the dawn, others join Carp and Ann, and we begin to discover what the situation is. Though the beginning is effective in catching our attention, more significant in illustrating Barker's skill is the absence of any formal, artificial exposition. We simply hear a group of people talking as they naturally would, with no obvious attempt made to give the audience the facts that they supposedly must know in order to understand the play. Barker does not depend here or in his later plays on old-fashioned devices like an older servant explaining things to a new one or a mother telling her daughter about other characters, which not even the supposedly skilled craftsman Pinero was above using. We learn soon enough that the kiss is Lord John's attempt to frighten Ann in order to win a wager with Mr. Tatton that Ann will be frightened by a walk in the garden in the dark.

Leete unexpectedly decides that his daughter has been compromised and challenges Lord John to a duel, which takes place off stage and in which Leete is slightly wounded. Lord John leaves, but he returns to ask Ann to marry him, with the idea that Leete will shift to his political party. This is the political alliance that Leete wants.

In the meantime, however, Ann has begun to think of her future and to grow up. Although brother George says to her, "Look upon yourself—not too seriously—Ann, as the instrument of political destiny," a bit later he advises her, on the contrary, to marry to please herself. Then we see various other forces working on Ann. John Abud has been cleverly and unobtrusively brought in near the end of act 1. He has come to begin his day's work as the others end their night's pleasure. In act 2 (later that day) he asks George about George's wife, Dolly, who is expecting a child. Ann remarks, "A baby is a wonderful thing." When Lord John returns to ask Ann to marry him, she finds him distasteful. "Why do you want to marry me?" she asks. "I love you," is his reply. She says, "It suddenly occurs to me that sounds unpleasant." Nevertheless she acts as if she would accept, though she says to her sister, "Sally, don't let me be forced to marry." A visit to Sarah from her husband's lawyer reminds Ann that Sarah's marriage has not worked out well. George questions Abud about his former interest in Dolly and advises him in Ann's presence that he should marry some decent woman—"we want gardeners." Ann, too, shows an interest in Abud's daily life and in whom he might marry.

Thus the various elements in the situation influence Ann to go against her father's wishes. In act 3 she refuses to accompany him to Brighton, where they are to meet Lord John again. "Sally must go back, for she belongs to it . .[2] but I'll stay here where I belong," she insists. "I mean to disobey you . . to stay here . . never to be un-happy." And she adds, "I want to be an ordinary woman . . not clever . . not fortunate." She says that she does not choose to become like her sister, and then suddenly, as Abud passes by, she asks him to marry her. In answer to the amazement of the others she explains simply, "Look . . he's straight-limbed and clear-eyed . . and I'm a woman."

In the last scene Ann and Abud enter their simple cottage after the wedding. They have walked the nine miles to it, and Ann is weary. They both wonder how their marriage will turn out. Ann says, "Well . . this is an experiment." Abud replies, "God help us both."

Ann's future will consist in scrubbing the floor and preparing meals for Abud. They agree each to do his part. Ann says in a comment which sums up the basic idea of the play: "Papa . . I said . . we've all been in too great a hurry getting civilised. False dawn. I mean to go back." And a moment later: "I was afraid to live . . and now . . I am content." The play ends as she opens the door to the stairs that lead up to the bedroom, and Abud lights the way up. Thus the Life Force, or nature, or the mating instinct, or eugenics has won out over political expediency, obedience to parent, and differences in social standing. Ann has behaved independently and unconventionally.

Some critics have felt that there is no satisfactory explanation for Ann's action in wanting to marry Abud.[3] That the marriage is not, however, completely unmotivated and inexplicable is clear from the skillful, if unobtrusive way in which Barker prepares for it. Ann herself may not be able to explain her choice, but Barker shows us the influences which cause her to prefer Abud over Lord John, whether Ann is herself completely aware of them or not.

The characterization in the play is intriguing. Ann is well portrayed, especially in the fact that she is not able to articulate the motives for her actions. Carnaby Leete is an excellent portrait. Though unscrupulous, he is not completely selfish, for in wanting Ann to marry Lord John he is thinking not only of his own gain but of the fact that after his death there will be nothing for her to live on. Sarah, though she has made a mistake in her own marriage, is clear-headed enough now to see the flaw in the whole Leete situation. "If we . . in this house I'm speaking of . . ," she says, "had made friends where we've only made tools and fools we shouldn't now be cursed as we are . . all."

Barker's experience in the theater undoubtedly helped him in creating scenes that are effective. The unusual opening is one; the scene of Ann's proposal to Abud is another. The scene in act 4 in which all of the relatives gather after the wedding is the first of Barker's several scenes depicting entire family groups with great vividness and ironic humor. *The Voysey Inheritance* and *The Madras House* each have such a scene. Here we have a meeting of three generations of a family and of two classes of society. Effective also is the final scene between the young couple. It is touching in its simplicity, in its suggestion of homely duties to be performed, in its glimmer of hope for the future.

The setting of the play is late eighteenth century, but whether Barker gives a faithful portrayal of the period is questionable. Indeed it does not seem that he has made any special attempt to suggest the eighteenth century in dialogue or characterization. Rather perhaps he has set the play a hundred years before his own time simply to point up what is essential—the decay of a family and the contrast between the marriage of convenience and the eugenic marriage. Actually Ann is the "modern" twentieth-century woman in contrast to the Victorian woman as much as, and perhaps more than, she is the "modern" nineteenth-century woman in contrast to the woman of the eighteenth century. The characters of Ann and Carnaby Leete are equally pertinent in either century.

Barker calls *The Marrying of Ann Leete* a comedy, and it is in some ways a comedy of manners. There are some witty lines suggestive of Oscar Wilde and of Shaw, especially at the beginning. For example, "Politics is a game for clever children, and women and fools." And: "Innocency's opinions are invariably entertaining." If it be a comedy of manners, it is also a problem play, though it does not take itself so seriously and is not so ponderous as most plays of this kind. Actually it treats more intellectually the problem of caste which Robertson dramatized very solemnly and melodramatically some years earlier (1867) and out of which Barrie was to make the more whimsical *Admirable Crichton* a short time later (1902). The play has also been called "our one genuine modern tragedy of manners."[4] It is, however, hardly a tragedy, for there is hope at the end. Ann is making a step in the right direction. She has asserted her independence. She is content. The devitalizing influence of convention has been swept away, and nature has won. The best description for *The Marrying of Ann Leete* is perhaps Meredithian comedy. It has the appeal to the intellect and the subtle delicacy which Meredith called for in his essay on *The Idea of Comedy* (published in 1897).

Concerned though it is with a real problem and realistic though it is in many ways (Tatton, for example, sits on the edge of a fountain in the dark and wets more than his coattails), yet *The Marrying of Ann*

Leete has a romantic quality of the dreamworld about it. It has been compared to the art of Turner and of Aubrey Beardsley in its strange, dreamy mood, a mood which continues and increases in *Prunella* and which Barker returns to later in *The Secret Life*. The dramatist creates a psychological atmosphere like Chekhov's in *The Cherry Orchard* and other plays and Shaw's in *Heartbreak House*,[5] both of which are later works. The dialogue has much to do with this mood of strangeness. It is not the commonplace speech of Galsworthy or Henry Arthur Jones, nor is it as witty as Shaw's. Undoubtedly the reason for its seeming obscurity at first reading is that the characters do not always answer one another logically and directly, especially at the beginning of the play. The play has also been described as a nocturne,[6] which it is in the superficial sense that much of it takes place at night, but it is by no means formless and sentimental. In some ways it suggests "modern" music—it is original, it does not have conventional harmonies, and it seems at first disjointed and unreal. But when one has listened for a time, clarity of form and strength and harmony appear. And there is all the more power in it for its original strangeness.

All critics agree that *The Marrying of Ann Leete* is a remarkable play for such a young man to have written. Nevertheless it must be admitted that it is not a complete success because of its relative obscurity, especially at the beginning. As one rereads the play, however, the original obscurity largely disappears and one is impressed by the fact that here is a carefully constructed, thoughtful, and vigorous work. Details fall into place. The very artificiality of the beginning is seen to suggest the life the characters are leading, while the simplicity of the last scene is similarly significant. Ann is both literally and figuratively in the dark at the beginning (even the candles carried by George are unlit), but at the end Abud lights her way up the stairs in the little cottage. Although it is only faint candlelight which she sees by, it is at least light to show her what is real and true.

From the point of view of Barker's subsequent development as a dramatist, *The Marrying of Ann Leete* is significant in revealing the combination of fancy and reality which he later succeeds in achieving also. It shows his interest in politics as the subject matter for drama and his concern with the problems of civilized society as they are faced by individual men and women. Not only does it promise greater things to come, but it is a lasting achievement in itself. John Palmer comments on the play's historical importance in a comparison: "Ann Leete lighted to her room in the fall of her wedding-day is, for the English theatre, a more precious and a more significant figure than Nora Helmer slamming the door upon *A Doll's House*. She is the woman of the future stage, who has found the world, in succession to the perturbing Helmers, who have lost it. She is the younger generation."[7] So with this, his first professionally produced and first published play, Granville Barker took his place with the group of new dramatists at the beginning of the twentieth century. With it he gave every indication of becoming one of the most important of these new dramatists in intellectual ability and theatrical skill.

Prunella

Whereas *The Marrying of Ann Leete* is an intellectual comedy, *Prunella* is a romantic fantasy. Written in 1902 in collaboration with Laurence Housman and first produced in 1904 at the Court Theatre, it was one of the most successful of the plays presented by the Vedrenne-Barker management. Both plays present rebellious heroines. Carnaby Leete says, "Nature's an encumbrance to us," but nonetheless in the course of the play nature wins a victory over too much civilization as Ann rebels against her father's wish to marry her off to a lord for his political advantage and instead marries a gardener. In *Prunella* the forces of civilization (a very straight-laced, conventional, narrow kind of civilization) are once again opposed to the forces of nature and once again nature wins as Prunella rebels against her strict upbringing and runs off with the irresponsible, lighthearted Pierrot.

The plot of the play is very simple. Prunella has been brought up by her maiden aunts, Privacy, Prim, and Prude, who have done their best to shelter her from the wicked outside world. She reads her lessons from *The Gentle Reader*, is ordered about by her aunts, and "deports" herself. Everything about the setting in the beginning symbolizes the restraints placed on nature by the well-meaning aunts. The garden is

enclosed by high, square-cut hedges. The house has "prim windows."
On the porch hangs a caged canary, symbolic of course of the heroine.
Three Gardeners are at work trimming the hedges; one of them tells
Prunella they are teaching nature to keep things under control. A Boy
shoos the naughty birds out of the garden. Only one object seems
somewhat out of place here—the statue of Love with viol and bow,
and this has its meaning, too. We learn from the Gardeners that the
"gardener architect" who erected it ran off some years ago with the
youngest sister of the family, who became Prunella's mother. Prunella herself was left in a basket at the door a year later, with a note
written by her mother just before her death identifying the baby. One
Gardener points out that Prunella is much like her mother and may
fall in love with the first handsome young man she sees. The aunts are
afraid that Prunella will catch sight of the mummers who are coming
to town, so they have ordered the blinds drawn and the garden gate
locked.

When the aunts hear the music of the mummers approaching, they
make the fatal error of running into the house and leaving Prunella to
pick up the lapful of needlework, thimbles, and scissors she has
dropped and to find the gate key which Privacy in her haste has let
fall. Into this little world of innocence Pierrot makes his way through
the bottom of the hedge, young and heedless of tomorrow in his
search for happiness here and now. He entices Prunella to run off with
him in act 2; she does so after the statue of Love in the garden says in
answer to her plea for advice, "Yea, harken to the lips of Love! /
Where he abideth all is well. . . ."

But to be true to his nature, Pierrot cannot be true to his Pierrette,
as he calls her. Three years have elapsed as act 3 opens. Two of the
aunts have died, and the third, Privacy, has just sold the house to a
gentleman who turns out to be Pierrot. We learn that having left
Pierrette after two years of joyful wandering together he returned to
find her gone. Since then he has been unable to be happy and has come
back again to the Dutch garden "to lay a ghost." By chance Prunella
herself returns to her old home at the same time, and she answers
Pierrot's wistful call for his Pierrette. Pierrot proves that he really
loves her after all, for though he thinks her a ghost and she says if he

but touch her he will become as she is, he goes to her. Birds sing once again, light glows, the statue of Love plays upon his viol, and the garden fills with song as the curtain falls.

In 1930 a new version of *Prunella* was published with an additional act inserted as act 3, the original act 3 becoming act 4. In the preface to the new version the authors explain that the new act has been added to make the play longer (apparently so that it can be presented without a companion piece) and to provide an opportunity for more stage effects. The act is a dramatization of Prunella's life with Pierrot and their separation after two years together.

The first scene in the new act is without dialogue. The mummers arrive on stage in a horse-drawn van—the horses are mummers with horse-figures around their waists—and put up for the night. Scaramel plays his guitar as lighting effects create the sunset. Then comes the sunrise, the characters awake, and the caravan departs.

In the second scene we see Prunella's unhappiness with their wandering life of make-believe and her yearning for a home. They rehearse a play for which Scaramel and the others prepare a setting of a mock Dutch garden with a statue of Luck caricaturing the statue of Love in the original garden of Prunella's aunts. Because Prunella refuses to go on with this kind of life, Pierrot leaves with the others and with a painted doll who has replaced Prunella in the play they perform. Prunella dons her old clothes to go home alone. Thus we see acted out what in the original version is only narrated. Otherwise the play remains the same.

Pierrot and Pierrette are the romantic element in the play. The other characters are more down-to-earth, though not necessarily realistic. The Gardeners furnish some rustic humor, as do the servants Queer and Quaint and the Boy who chases away the birds and later becomes the "'ead Gardener." Pierrot has a flock of rowdy companions—Hawk, Kennel, Callow, Mouth, Doll, Romp, Tawdry, Coquette, who are not individually much characterized, as their names would indicate. Pierrot's servant, Scaramel, is one of the most interesting persons in the play. He is worldly wise, cynical, fully aware of his master's activities and propensities, but completely faithful to him. When, after meeting Prunella, Pierrot muses in the garden that he is tempted, Scaramel replies, "Always yield to temptation." He believes that love ought not to be taken seriously, that it never lasts. He thinks it foolish of Pierrot to have come back to the garden and even to remember Pierrette.

But Pierrot does remember this time. Though he tries to be gay, his friends look old and ugly to him and he is troubled by the thought of poor Pierrette. So in act 3 we get the moral (really the second one) of the play. If it is wrong to try to keep love out of one's life and to live according to rules and in seclusion from emotion, so also is it wrong to live and love selfishly. Pierrot learns that that is not the way to happiness. Thus *Prunella* turns out to be actually a moral allegory in the guise of fantasy.

Though the ending, in which the lovers are happily reunited after Pierrot has proved his love, has been criticized as not in keeping with the Pierrot character, the play is charming. The satiric touches in the aunts and in Prunella's education are gently effective. There is beauty in the love scenes, and a delicate moonlight atmosphere bathes the entire play. Music has a large part in the overall effect; indeed Barker's production of the play was an excellent example of the happy union of all the arts of the theater—acting, poetry, costumes, lighting, scenery, and music. In its skillful construction as well as its masterly combination of appeal to eye, ear, heart, and mind, *Prunella* shows in scene after scene the skill of the man who had firsthand experience with the theater.

Obviously in reading a play, especially one like *Prunella*, one needs to use imagination to supply all of the details of color, movement, music, and the warmth of human voice and presence which are provided in the theatrical presentation. Unfortunately the book version of this play is rather tame and colorless, and for this the dialogue is largely to blame. It is written in a combination of prose and verse, used with no evident discrimination. The prose is found when it apparently was not convenient to express the ideas in rhyme, and the verse seldom rises to poetry. It is mainly in uninspired rhymed couplets (chiefly pentameter, occasionally tetrameter and trimeter) with some very awkward rhymes. The dialogue may have been successful in the theater, but in printed form it is flat.

The work being a collaboration, it is interesting to speculate as to which qualities and details are the contribution of each of the authors, though it can never be known with certainty. The verse has been credited to Housman and the construction and the disillusioned Scaramel character to Barker.[8] This division of credit is based on several facts. Housman wrote other poetry; Barker's only other verse is in "A Miracle," an unpublished one-act play.[9] Housman wrote a later play, *Moonshine* (published in 1922), in which a different kind of Pierrot appears and the Scaramel character does not; and the intellectual, worldly-wise qualities of Scaramel are in keeping with those of other Barker characters. This is perhaps as far as one can go in throwing light on the collaboration. Housman himself stated that when people asked what he and Barker each contributed, "I can only truthfully tell them that in that happy collaboration the yard measure has no place, and the only fact which mattered was that his joint authorship made the play twice as good as it would otherwise have been."[10]

The program of the first production of *Prunella* described it as "A Play, in Three Acts, for Grown-up Children."[11] A play for children it may be in its fantasy and imaginative qualities and tone of unreality. But *Prunella* has, in addition to its charm and sentiment, intellectual and moral characteristics which give it a deeper significance than at first it may seem to possess. In it the seriousness of the actual world is most happily united with the atmosphere of the dreamworld. The play shows a different aspect of the elements of unreality and fancy which are found, especially in the beginning, in *The Marrying of Ann Leete*, a more childlike, fairy-tale kind of unreality; and it shows again Barker's concern with the fundamental problems of life, which no true artist can for long escape. *Prunella* shows, too, that once again Barker had the originality and courage to depart from the conventional commercial type of play, and the skill to make that departure successful.

Chapter Four

Heroes with Problems: *The Voysey Inheritance* and *Waste*

Though unquestionably a remarkable play to be written by a young man, *The Marrying of Ann Leete* is nevertheless a promise of greatness to come rather than a completely satisfactory expression of that greatness. *Prunella*, though charming and theatrically effective, is not a serious drama and is, moreover, not Barker's work alone. It is in *The Voysey Inheritance* that Barker achieved his first maturely forceful work in his career as a playwright, and in *Waste* he continued to fulfill his promise. Both of these plays are excellent examples of realism-naturalism in theme, settings, characterization, and objectivity of presentation.

The Voysey Inheritance

In *The Voysey Inheritance* Barker uses a theme that dramatists have found profitable in various ways through the centuries, from Shakespeare in *King Lear* to Pinero in *The Thunderbolt*. But Barker's original-ity is evident in that the Voysey inheritance is different from any other. It is not a fortune but rather the serious problem of the dishonesty with which the elder Voysey has for years been carrying on his business. Intrusted as a family solicitor with various investments for his clients, he has not been faithful or honest toward them but has instead used their capital to try to make money for himself while continuing to pay the expected interest to his clients. At the begin-ning of the play, Edward, his son, has just been told the true state of affairs. The father wants him to carry on until the accounts have all been put straight, which, he says, is what he has been striving to do. Voysey explains that this was his inheritance from his father and that Edward will be his heir. Not much later the elder Voysey dies, and Edward does indeed inherit this long continued dishonest conduct of trusts. Barker then presents in the major portion of the play, for the most part in a very convincing fashion, the moral dilemma in which Edward finds himself, the reactions of the other members of the family, and the final outcome.

Perhaps the influence of Shaw can be seen in the fundamental moral question which the play poses—the question of compromising one's principles in an effort to do good. Like Trench in *Widowers' Houses* and Vivie in *Mrs. Warren's Profession*, Edward Voysey is faced with the problem of compromising with evil. Barker, however, treats it in a different way from Shaw. In *Widowers' Houses*, Trench, at first shocked to find that his fiancée's money comes from slum landlordism, then learns that his own income is from the same source. He compromises with his principles in order to keep his income and to win back his fiancée. Vivie, in *Mrs. Warren's Profession*, does not compromise, however, when she learns where the money her mother is giving her comes from. She makes a clean break from her mother and earns her own living honorably and independently, though Mrs. Warren and her profession continue to flourish. For Edward Voysey the problem is more complex.

The idealistic Edward has always admired his father and trusted him. When he learns the horrible truth about his father's seeming prosperity, he is torn between two emotions—honor, and love of father. He decides to stay with the business because he really cannot leave his father in his difficulties and because possibly he can see to it that some of the wrongs are righted. But the dishonest situation troubles him greatly. Then the elder Voysey dies, and Edward plans to reveal the truth about the whole mess and take whatever punishment may come. When he enlightens the rest of the family as to the actual source of their money, they are not so shocked or even surprised as he has expected. Mrs. Voysey has known for some time and has feared that the break would come during her husband's lifetime. The eldest son, Trenchard, has suspected for some time. Edward sincerely believes that they should give up all they have to set the wrong right, though even only a partial restitution could be made. No one else is so idealistic, however, and Edward finds himself disillusioned in his family. They are all concerned with their own selfish interests and refuse to sacrifice anything, even though their money has been fraudulently obtained. Even Alice Maitland, a cousin with whom Edward is in love, wants him to carry on his father's business and quietly try to set right the small accounts of those to whom a loss would be tragic.

And so, after some deliberation, Edward takes up the burden of the inheritance with the intention of doing moral right by committing legal wrong. But at least he does not continue making illicit profits out of his clients and manages to put some of the smaller accounts into shape before one day George Booth, an old friend of the family, decides to take his business away from the firm since he does not trust Edward as much as he trusted his father. Booth is told the truth, and it seems as if the crash has finally come. When Booth, after some thought, suggests that he will not prosecute if Edward continues paying him his income and gradually makes good on his capital, Edward simply laughs at him. The play ends before we find out whether Edward is going to be released from his inheritance, which is what he would like, by being prosecuted. In the meantime, however, some good has come from it to Edward. He has won the heart of Alice by becoming in her eyes more of a man and less of a prig.

Though Edward is very well characterized, Alice Maitland is the least convincing person in the play. She is an example of the "new woman," and through her Barker expresses some of the Shavian and Fabian ideas which have become his, too. For example, Alice believes that the money which has been lost, by some of the clients at least, was never theirs by right anyhow. She does, however, feel sorry for the poorer people who will be beggared by their loss. Practical in her own outlook on life, she thinks this difficulty will be a blessing to Edward in forcing him to be practical. She says that because Edward is not pleased by the things of this world he withdraws from it, but one must not despise practical things, and one must not neglect one's happiness. Encouraged by Alice, Edward proposes to her once again, and she accepts. She has an income of her own and wants them to start life on that. She demands to be treated as his equal, though really she seems the stronger of the two. Thus far we may accept Alice as a convincing portrait, especially of the "new woman." When at the end, however, Alice says that if Edward is imprisoned she will be proud of him and completely ignores the fact that they may well be separated from one another for some time, she goes too far in her intellectuality to be a completely convincing woman in love. Indeed the love affair between the hero and the heroine is strangely unemotional and unsatisfying throughout. There is a superhuman quality about Alice and a complete certainty of herself that are not very attractive. Her intellect invariably dominates her heart.

The most fascinating character in the play is the elder Voysey himself. Ibsen's portrait of the ruined financial giant John Gabriel Borkman had already appeared in 1897, but Voysey's likeness to him is only very superficial. Barker's skill shows itself in the brilliant way in which Voysey's character is revealed a little at a time until we get the complete picture. He tells Edward at the beginning that he inherited the deficit from his father and that the dishonest conduct of the firm has been going on for more than thirty years. He is vague about how bad things were when he came into control, but he gains sympathy by suggesting that he could not simply allow his father to lose his good name and the clients their money without trying to do something. And now, he says, the firm's name is unblemished. Voysey has great confidence in his own investment skill—that, he asserts, is the security his clients have for their money. He insists that it would be cowardly of Edward to flee from the responsibility of carrying on the business in the same way. He believes that following one's own idea of right and wrong is more commendable than obeying the law, and he has found happiness in this sort of dangerous life.

At first one has a sort of admiration for the buccaneering Voysey's courage, strength, and skill in a difficult situation. He seems almost heroic while he is actually present and we get the full force of his personality, but further light thrown on his character after his death modifies our impression. Edward discovers that his father was even less noble than he at first thought. Finding only one irregularity that is more than ten years old, and that in old Booth's account, Edward then believes that Voysey's story about his father having started the dishonesty is a fiction. Trenchard's suggestion that this tale shows the artist in the criminal reminds us that the elder Voysey regularly brought roses to the office and artistically arranged them himself, putting one in his buttonhole. Thus Barker cleverly ties in seemingly insignificant details. Now Edward believes that Voysey told him about his illegal practices at least partly for the satisfaction of having someone know about his cleverness.

But the picture is not even yet complete. Peacey, the faithful old employee in the firm, tells Edward that Voysey apparently was unable to give up the excitement of the game, for he once had things in perfect order only to start again. Another bit of damning evidence is introduced against Voysey when old Booth tells Edward that he had decided more than a year before Voysey's death that he could not let Edward have complete control over his affairs as he had allowed his father to, and that though he never specifically said so to Voysey, Voysey might easily have surmised it. Startled, Edward shrinks from the disturbing implications of this possibility and refuses to accept it.

Thus even after his death (which occurs between acts 2 and 3) the figure of the elder Voysey is kept before us to fascinate us constantly. At the very end of the play Barker in a stage direction calls our attention to him for the final time. Now that Edward has become a human being, has shown some courage, and has won Alice's approval, the elder Voysey looks down at his son from his portrait over the mantelpiece with kindness but still with the suggestion of the buccaneer in his eyebrows. The characterization of the elder Voysey is an outstanding accomplishment.

Although the Voyseys, father and son, and Alice are the three chief characters in the play, there are a host of others, all of whom are quite completely individualized. Edward's brothers—pompous, conceited, not very bright Booth; artistic Hugh; Trenchard, a barrister, cool and confident—all are different and yet recognizable as members of the same family. Ethel, the youngest child, is spoiled and says, more seriously than not, that her father has no better use for his money than to spend it on her. Honor, the unmarried elder daughter, is mother's helper, imposed on by everyone.

The scene (act 3) in which Edward confronts the whole family with the news about their father's dishonesty is remarkable. Booth deplores Edward's lack of reverence in wanting to talk about money right after the funeral, but in the very same breath he asks if Trenchard is getting some lunch. When he is made to realize the full import of the news, he is concerned first about the family's finances and second about the family honor—that is, honor in the eyes of the world. He is not worried about the clients' losses and is quite happy to accept Trenchard's opinion that there is no reason, legal or moral, for the family to give up their money. Hugh, vague and impractical, meanwhile wonders if Voysey is eavesdropping on them from wherever he is. This scene is certainly the best that Barker had written up to this time, if not the best in all his work. He succeeds in creating individuals and in suggesting various shades of meaning with regard to the whole moral problem.

Like *The Marrying of Ann Leete*, this play is very carefully integrated. Details which seem insignificant at the time—Voysey's roses, for example—come to have meaning, often ironical, later on. Old Booth early in the play accuses Edward of creating problems. He maintains that young people can ask the advice of their elders, and adults have laws, man-made and divine, to show them the way. He is quite satisfied with his life and has never needed more than five minutes to make up his mind about anything important. Yet when Edward later tells him that half his money is gone, Booth is pathetic in his indecision. What should he do? Why should he have to make a decision? Cannot Edward give him the answer?

The influence of Shaw and of Socialism may be detected in *The Voysey Inheritance* in the considerable criticism of society, especially the English middle class, which is scattered throughout the play, though Barker is not necessarily always in agreement with what some of his characters say. Underlying the whole play is the idea that too much emphasis is placed on money and on the appearance of wealth and respectability. For example, when Voysey tells Edward that he has earned the trust of his clients by his aura of financial success, Edward retorts, "Not our worth, not our abilities, nor our virtues, but the fact that we travel first class and in hansoms." Hugh blasts a society that leaves its streets and its children filthy, where people are educated to "believe in the Laws and the Money-market and Respectability." He insists that "vitality" is more important than money, and wants to give up his money in order to learn his real worth as a person.

Beatrice, a "new woman" and a writer, who has married Hugh for money and now wants a divorce, reveals much the same attitude as Hugh toward the middle class. Edward agrees with her sarcasm about the middle class, but he cannot agree with her praise of Voysey's imagination in robbing his smug clients of their unearned money. She points out, however, that he has been doing the same thing now.

Shavian though all this social criticism may sound, it is expressed in speeches which are natural in style rather than being operatic arias like so many of Shaw's, and there is a difference in tone between the two dramatists. Shaw seems frequently flippant and always very sure of himself. His plays have been criticized as having been written for the main purpose of expounding his ideas about life and society, and his characters have been called (certainly not always with justice) mere mouthpieces for these ideas. We tend to be conscious of Shaw's wit at times rather than of the personalities of the speakers themselves. Barker is less witty and less certain of what is right and wrong. He examines problems through individualized characters in concrete situations, and although his plays contain an abundance of ideas they are ideas which seem to come from the characters and are consistent with them rather than being the brilliant thoughts of the author himself.

The real Barker philosophy in *The Voysey Inheritance* is expressed by Alice. Incidentally, the women in this play are generally superior to the men in intellectual strength, courage, and culture—evidence of the continued emancipation of women in drama since Nora Helmer banged the door on Torvald. Alice, quite the most cool, collected, and confident person in the play, very ably evaluates the situation at the end. It does not matter what happens to Edward now, she believes, for having eliminated all selfishness and therefore having nothing to fear or to hope for, he is in control. Though he would like to have his fate definitely decided, Alice suggests that he might well wish to continue the uncertain state of affairs for the rest of his life. "My dear, the world must be put tidy," she tells him. "That's the work which splendid criminals . . and others leave for us poor commonplace people to do." The play ends with Alice reminding Edward, who does not believe in an afterlife, that they have their life here on earth to look forward to.

Thus Barker has shown us that there are rich fools who have not earned their money, there are poor people who must be helped, there are ineffectual social malcontents like Hugh and able people hardened by life's adversities like Beatrice, there are clever criminals like the elder Voysey, and there are idealists who have courage and strength like Edward and Alice (especially Alice, who gives strength to the man she loves). It is in these idealists that the hope of the world lies, for they have learned, like Edward, that nobler than individual freedom is an altruistic acceptance of the demands of service to society—which acceptance alone gives one true freedom.

The fact that the play seems unresolved at the end has troubled some critics, early ones more so than later. Desmond MacCarthy, for example, complains that it is a flaw typical of the new dramatists, of whom Barker is one, to end the play before we find out what is to happen to Edward; our curiosity should be satisfied.[1] Later critics are more likely to have been content to accept the development of Edward's character as the subject of the play. Graham Sutton, for example, says: ". . . The spiritual conflict is complete, the material issue is rightly left uncertain."[2] This change in the attitude of the critics may be some measure of the influence of Barker and the other "new" dramatists on playwriting, for after their work a play no longer had to concern itself with primarily a series of physical actions; mental or spiritual action was recognized as properly dramatic. Of course the ending is not really completely inconclusive. There is a good chance that Edward will not be accused and imprisoned, but if he should be, we know that he can now accept his fate with stoic fortitude. The ending of this play, like that of *The Marrying of Ann Leete*, shows the naturalistic quality of suggesting not termination but the continuation of life after the curtain falls.

Although *The Voysey Inheritance* is predominantly serious in tone, it does not lack satirically humorous touches. Old Booth and Booth Voysey are both made foolish in their pompous self-righteousness and hypocrisy. Mrs. Voysey, hard of hearing, lives in a world pretty much apart from the present and furnishes some unconsciously ironic remarks. She reads about the Cromwell family—good blood but somehow some bad got in; soon after Hugh has lambasted the British Empire for its faults, Mrs. Voysey finishes an article about the

Chinese Empire, which she concludes must be in a frightful condition. Most effectively the humor in the work arises not from any farcical actions or artificial wit but largely from the characters' unawareness of themselves.

Though Barker in this play is like Shaw in that he writes a conversational play rather than one filled with action, *The Voysey Inheritance* is in no sense an imitation of anything else. The realism in characterization, settings, and dialogue (with the possible exception of the more Shavian speeches of Alice) places the work in the mainstream of realism which had been growing in the drama of the period, and the work in itself was an influence toward that realism. Henderson points out that "the professional playgoer wants 'the same old game' year after year—romantic love, thrills, *scènes à faire*, 'curtains,' dramatic tangles dexterously unwound, handsome men and beautiful women, exquisite scenery, magnificent costumes."[3] This is exactly what Barker, in his attempts to write intelligent mature drama, does not want. A mature, thought-provoking, and yet entertaining play is what Barker produced in *The Voysey Inheritance*.

As *The Marrying of Ann Leete* was likened to the landscapes of Turner, so this play has been compared to Rembrandt and Franz Hals,[4] with something of Hogarth's "brutality" and "vigor."[5] Compared to *Ann Leete*, it has the virtue of being less cloudy and easier to understand. William Archer tells us that he had read several of Barker's youthful plays in manuscript and had been unable to understand them. Barker then said "he would write one down to my intelligence." The result was *The Marrying of Ann Leete*, which, however, Archer still found to be "enigmatic." But the afternoon of November 7, 1905, when he saw *The Voysey Inheritance*, he calls "a red-letter day in my own experience; for on that afternoon I realised (utterly against all expectation or hope) that I could actually understand and enjoy a play by Mr. Granville-Barker." It was not simply a play that could be understood, continues Archer, but "a great play, a play conceived and composed with original mastery, and presenting on its spacious canvas a greater wealth of observation, character and essential drama than was to be found in any other play of our time." This high opinion of Barker's talent was confirmed for Archer by his next two plays, *Waste* and *The Madras House*. "I do not hesitate to say that I consider these three plays the biggest things our modern movement has produced."[6]

Barker revised *The Voysey Inheritance* in 1913. He changed none of its essentials, but he did alter the phrasing of lines here and there to make them smoother and he changed a few of the Shavian remarks of Alice and Hugh to eliminate something of the preaching effect of the original version.

Waste

The success which Granville Barker achieved with *The Voysey Inheritance* in writing intelligent realistic drama of lasting literary value as well as theatrical effectiveness he continued to find in his next work, *Waste*, written in 1906—1907.

In *Waste*, a powerful problem play with a tragic outcome, Barker returns to the idea of the Life Force or nature in opposition to the conventions of society. But whereas in *The Marrying of Ann Leete* the Life Force brought together two young people and ended on a note of hope for the future in the prospect of their having children who would be strong and healthy, in *Waste* the persons who are joined (and only for a brief half-hour of sex) are older—one a brilliant, cold politician of forty-five and the other a shallow, selfish, though charming, married woman. The result for the woman is the loss of her life through an abortion because she lacks the courage to give birth to their child, and for the man the loss of his chance to bring to fruition a political plan the success of which is his greatest desire and the loss of his life through suicide.

The basic situation of a scandal in the life of a prominent politician and his consequent loss of power suggests the cases of Sir Charles Dilke, a well-known member of the Liberal party who in 1885 was named co-respondent in a divorce suit and who thereafter, though the case against him was dismissed, retired from politics; and of Charles Parnell, who because of his love affair with Mrs. Katie O'Shea lost his leadership of the Irish party in 1890. William Archer says that Barker got the idea for the plot of *Waste* from neither of these real-life situations, however, but from the suicide of a soldier whom Margery M. Morgan identifies as Major-General Sir Hector MacDonald, who shot himself when his career was placed in jeopardy because of scandal.[7] Any similarity to real persons or happenings is, nonetheless, merely superficial. In the course of the four acts of his play Barker presents a realistic drama combined with a commentary on society's waste of a talented public figure because of the commission of an act in his private life.

The fact that *Waste* refers to an illegal operation—the word "abortion" is never used in the play—caused it originally to be refused public performance by the Lord Chamberlain. Thus the play was first produced "privately" on November 24, 1907, by the Stage Society, a so-called "private" performance not requiring approval by the Lord Chamberlain.[8] Certainly there is today nothing sensational in the dialogue of the play; and the ending would satisfy the demands of the strictest moralist, for both sinners are punished by suffering and death.

When this play and Edward Garnett's *The Breaking Point* were banned in 1907, the whole question of censorship in England was brought to the fore. Seventy-one literary men signed a protest against the prevailing practice, among them the foremost writers of the day—Barker, Barrie, Conrad, Galsworthy, Gilbert, Hankin, Hardy, Henry James, H. A. Jones, Masefield, Meredith, Gilbert Murray, Pinero, Shaw, Swinburne, and Arthur Symons.[9] The incident helped bring about an investigation of the censorship by a parliamentary committee in 1909. Thus Barker by writing *Waste* incidentally performed an unintentional service to the English theater, for some modifications in the censorship were made as a result of the report of this committee.[10] In 1920 *Waste* was licensed with no alterations,[11] though it was not publicly performed until December 1, 1936, in a revised version.[12]

The center of the drama is Henry Trebell, an important politician who has withdrawn his support from the Radicals to help the Tories into power with the intent of getting passed a Disestablishment Bill and embarking on a grand educational scheme with the money to be gained as a result of disestablishment. Trebell is sincere, intelligent, and forward-looking, but he feels superior to and aloof from the rest of mankind. Though he works for the good of society, he has been a member of no party, for he prizes his independence and his power over others. He has found no woman with both charm and brains and so has never married. His sister says he pays no attention to women, but in the light of what happens that is hardly a completely accurate statement. Amy O'Connell, the married woman who becomes pregnant by him, accuses him of wanting imagination, of not developing his highest potential, and of being self-satisfied. He, however, feels that self-development is a waste of time and that he is no more self-satisfied "than any machine that runs smoothly."

Barker presents Trebell in some discussions about education and religion which are interesting in themselves and because they reveal Trebell's character. He believes that in religion neither the supernatural nor Christian dogma is necessary, that education will be the religion of the future and teachers the priests. These teachers must, however, be of a new type, not "text-book teachers" but learners themselves, always seeking the truth and striving to communicate it, and thus serving God. He is optimistic about the future. "I have only one belief myself," he states. "That is in human progress. . . ." This is the strong, thoughtful man whose life is ruined by his own momentary physical desire and by the weakness of a woman.

The woman is not without blame in the original act of sin. Amy confesses that ever since they first met three months ago, she has been determined to get closer to him. When Trebell kisses her, they are both swept into the full current of the Life Force. Amy is completely self-centered. She does not live with her husband because she does not want children. Learning that she is to have a child by Trebell, her one thought is to prevent such an occurrence. When in act 2 she confronts Trebell with the news in their first meeting after that night (he has been on the Continent for some weeks), she is petulant because he does not say he loves her; he honestly admits he never has. Though he does not want to marry her, for they are not in love and would not get along, he does offer to help her and wants to take care of the child if she will not. He feels that now for the first time she has acquired some importance because she is serving a purpose in this world, but she is afraid and feels very sorry for herself. She insists that she will not have the child, not because of possible scandal but because she simply is afraid of bearing it. Before they can decide what is to be done, they are interrupted, and though Trebell begs her to wait she leaves and has the abortion which ends the child's life and hers as well.

Barker's presentation of this age-old situation of adultery and an illegitimate child is completely different from the usual sentimental version. One is made to feel little sympathy for Amy, even though Trebell admittedly is rather cold toward her plight when he suddenly learns of it. The whole treatment of the love affair is different from that in romantic fiction and drama. Indeed there is no love affair. Amy has flirted with fire and got burned. She has known all along that Trebell is not in love with her, nor she with him. There is not even the consolation of an ennobling emotion between them to compensate for their deaths.

Some critics have found Trebell a totally unsympathetic character. Henderson, for example, calls him "repellent and abnormal in temperament; a megalomaniac of the most virulent type," with "no spark of altruism" in his personality, "a monster."[13] True enough, Trebell shows little feeling toward Amy when he learns of her condition. It is an understandable coldness, however, especially in view of her attitude. True enough, there is an intellectual austerity about Trebell, and overly great self-sufficiency, but at the end of the play he protests to his sister, Frances, that though he has never been concerned in a narrow sense with individuals, only impersonally with broader issues, he has never thought selfishly. Hardhearted though he is, Trebell is very much affected by the thought of his child and deeply wounded by its loss. "The man bears the child in his soul," he says, "as the woman carries it in her body." This portrayal of the desire of the man for a child is different from Shaw's view that the man is unwillingly forced into being the means of nature's insistence on procreation.

In act 3 an informal cabinet meeting is held which is as skillfully written as the scene of the family conclave in *The Voysey Inheritance*. The dialogue holds one's interest and the individualization of the characters and the understanding of human nature shown are superb. William Archer calls this scene "the highest point yet reached in modern English drama."[14] This meeting decides that Trebell, because of his involvement with Amy, will not be asked to serve in the cabinet. The decision leads to his suicide.

In the last act of the play, Barker creates a scene more moving than any he had heretofore achieved. The solicitude of Trebell's sister,

Frances, his own feeling of defeat and frustration, his recognition of
the fact that Frances has not had an easy life with him, his feeling for
his unborn child—all these details help to humanize the political
machine that he has been. Barker builds up the atmosphere of doom
most effectively. Trebell's life is at an end, though Frances does not
believe he will end it. He kills himself partly to make those politicians
who now will not have him in the cabinet think, partly because he
will not be able to advance his ideas in the cabinet, and partly (mostly,
perhaps) because he feels deeply the loss of his unborn child. In a sense
Barker has prepared for Trebell's death as early as his first description
of Trebell's sensitive mouth. Try as he may, Trebell is unable to
suppress emotion completely and to control himself entirely by
reason.

After Trebell's death, his secretary, Walter Kent, makes the final
comment on the situation: "I'm angry . . just angry at the waste of a
good man. Look at the work undone . . think of it! Who is to do it!
Oh . . the waste . . !" The waste has been caused by Trebell's own
nature, by Amy's weakness, and by the short-sightedness of society
itself.

Powerful though the play is, it is not without some weaknesses.
The opening scene presents us with a roomful of characters talking in
a realistic fashion; out of this talk we gain the necessary information
about Trebell and the political situation without being conscious of
hearing exposition. But the dialogue is difficult to follow for a while.
In the love scene in act 1 the passion between the lovers is not made
quite convincing enough; to a degree they are merely puppets in the
hands of the playwright. In the cabinet meeting scene Barker uses
the flimsy device of a new servant getting his people and his orders
confused to bring two of the characters into the room accidentally—
Trebell, whose fate is being discussed, and O'Connell, the wronged
husband.

Some critics have objected to the political discussion in the play as
being too lengthy, dull, and irrelevant. [15] Although one can see why
these discussions might at first seem extraneous, actually they are not,
for the realm of activity (and talk) that Trebell is most vitally
interested in is politics. The plot element between Amy and Trebell is
really important only for its effect on Trebell's career and personality.

In this play, as almost invariably in Barker, the action is mainly internal rather than physical. The act of suicide of the hero, for example, is not shown, only the result.

In 1926 Barker entirely revised *Waste*, and a comparison of the two versions of the play is interesting from the point of view of the development of the dramatist. The characters, events, and basic theme remain the same, but the weaknesses in the earlier version are eliminated. The opening dialogue, for example, is shortened and made clearer. The love scene between Amy and Trebell is made much more convincing. Instead of having known each other for three months, they have first met a year ago or more. There is much less intellectual talk between them before he kisses her, the first kiss now takes place on stage rather than off, and more kisses follow. The act ends not with Trebell carrying Amy off into the darkness in a burst of animal passion, but with the more comfortable if less dashing prospect of his going to her room. In act 3 the awkward device of the bungling servant originally used to bring Trebell and O'Connell unexpectedly face to face is changed. There are no accidents; instead Trebell forces his way into the room because he wants to confront the husband of the dead woman. The motivation for Trebell's suicide is somewhat altered. There is no longer an emphasis on his sense of personal loss as a father in the death of the child, but rather on his loss of the great opportunity to do some good as a politician, to fulfill the purpose to which he has given himself completely and which he recognizes as something bigger than he is. This change is for the better; the original stress on Trebell's sudden sense of fatherhood is perhaps a bit strained. Barker improves the dialogue throughout by making it smoother, easier to follow, and less didactic in tone. All in all, the revised version is more powerful than the original.

Waste on the whole is more intellectual than emotional in its content and appeal, the earlier version especially. In the lack of emotional uplift at the end and in the part played by social environment in bringing about the ending it resembles many of its realistic modern successors in the genre of tragedy. As a modern tragedy it is sincere and successful. In fact, Archer went so far as to call it "our greatest modern tragedy."[16] Trebell is a fine conception of the tragic hero in the Greek sense, too: he is an important figure in the state for whom things are prospering until he is thwarted by fate and by the flaw in his own character.

With this, the fourth of his professionally produced and published plays, Granville Barker demonstrates again that he is a versatile and highly original dramatist. If there are influences on this work, they are influences only in a very general and superficial way. Martin Ellehauge in comparing *Waste* with Wedekind's *Frühlingserwachen*, which deals with similar material, points out that the differences are great. In Barker there is little of Wedekind's compassion for the woman involved; rather she is censured for her weakness.[17] Once again, as in *The Voysey Inheritance*, we see Shaw's interest in social criticism, but again, unlike Shaw, instead of expounding his own ideas through the characters and being absolutely certain that he is right, Barker is interested in the people themselves and examines life from various points of view, commenting on faults in society, to be sure, but not writing for the sake of supplying his own infallible remedies. In his balanced presentation of more than one side to a question, Barker resembles Galsworthy, but the social forces and opposing ideas which Galsworthy emphasizes are in Barker combined with and outweighed by forces of personality. Moreover, his plays are more complex than Galsworthy's and his dialogue is on a more intellectual level. In the fact that Barker allows "no romance . . . between the sexes, no sentimentalism," he may be "too docile a pupil of . . . Shaw," as W. L. Courtney suggests,[18] but more likely, since he treated the marriage of Ann Leete in the same unsentimental way, he is just being himself. Like Milton, who benefited from his contact with parliamentary affairs in creating his great meeting of the fallen angels in Hell, Barker probably gained knowledge of politics from his interest in Socialism and his association with Shaw and Webb. In his wisdom in seeing, despite all his intellectualism, that there is something more to life and its laws than mere intellect, something not easily defined but nonetheless important, he is following, if anyone, masters earlier than Shaw.

Waste, continuing the theme of nature in conflict with reason and with convention which appeared in *The Marrying of Ann Leete*, shows clearly that Barker has matured as a man and a dramatist in the seven or eight years that passed between the writing of the two plays. More than that, it is a play which can stand on its own merits and challenge comparison with any serious play of its period. Even without the notoriety of being banned by the censor, it would have established Barker in the forefront of the new dramatists in England.

Chapter Five

The Woman Question and Others: *The Madras House, The Harlequinade,* and Short Plays

The Madras House

From the unrelieved gloom of *Waste* Granville Barker turned to a totally different type of play. *The Madras House* (written in 1909 and produced in 1910) he calls a comedy, and a true comedy it is in the best Meredithian sense of arousing thoughtful laughter. It is nevertheless fundamentally a serious play, for Barker is concerned throughout with the tremendously big "woman problem"—the place of woman in society and the relationship between the sexes; and in the course of the play he presents various phases of this question. In a sense then this play is a continuation of the theme with which he started his dramatic career in *The Marrying of Ann Leete.* In structure and technique, however, *The Madras House* is different from all of Barker's earlier plays, so different indeed that it has been condemned as not a play at all. The episodes are unified simply in these ways: the hero, Philip Madras, appears in each one; they are all concerned with characters associated with the coutourier's establishment known as the Madras House or its companion drapery firm of Roberts and Huxtable; and they all deal with some aspect of the theme of the play. The ending is less conclusive than the ending of *The Voysey Inheritance*: the curtain is closed as Philip and his wife are discussing their relationship, but as the dramatist says in his final stage direction, *"She doesn't finish, for really there is no end to the subject."*

In the first act Barker presents one aspect of the woman question in the form of satire on the English middle class. Mr. Huxtable, surviving partner in the firm of Roberts and Huxtable, has a wife and six unmarried daughters. He is a well-meaning, rather meek man; Mrs. Huxtable is dignified and domineering; and the six daughters (ranging in age from thirty-nine down to twenty-six), are, Barker says, as alike one another as lead pencils, differing only in size and sharpness. The ugly Huxtable drawing-room is described as the "family museum." Mr. Huxtable expresses the wish to retire to have leisure to read the books he has been collecting in fine editions for years.

Of the daughters only the youngest has ever been proposed to, and then the young man was found not good enough for her. Mrs. Huxtable has decided that her "daughters should be sought after for themselves alone. That should ensure their happiness. Any eligible young man who visits here constantly is always given to understand, delicately, that nothing need be expected from Mr. Huxtable beyond his approval." And in the same breath she shows her delicacy by innocently remarking to a visitor, "You a r e married, I think you said, Major Thomas." Emma Huxtable tells cousin Philip Madras that the girls would be unappreciative of their good home if they were not happy. Yet sister Julia has kept a man's collar that came by mistake from the laundry, and Emma admits that they quarrel at times. Emma explains that the girls are always occupied: "I mean there's lots to be done about the house and there's calling and classes and things." Philip suggests that they all go away from home but is stumped when Emma asks, "Where to?"

There is a great deal of satiric humor in the feeble attempts of the Huxtables to make conversation with Philip and his friend Major Thomas. Introductions repeated to the various daughters, chants of "How d'you do?", and comments on the view of the Crystal Palace are hilariously prominent in the dialogue, along with embarrassed pauses, questions, and shifts of subject until the act fades out in a chorus of good-byes.

Not the least entertaining bits in this act are the pointed and revealing comments the author makes in his stage directions. For example, when Julia leaves the room, Mrs. Huxtable questions where she is going. Barker explains: *"When they were quite little girls Mrs. Huxtable always did ask her daughters where they were going when they left the room and where they had been when they entered it and she has never dropped the habit. They resent it only by the extreme patience of their replies."* Clara and Jane disagree about their being able to enjoy the garden next door. Says Barker: *"This stimulating difference of opinion takes them to the balcony."* And here is his description of the dinner gong: *"A tremendous gong, beloved of the English middle class, which makes any house seem small. A hollow sound: the dinner hour striking its own empty stomach."* For the full effect of the irony and humor in this scene and the only slightly exaggerated realism one must read the whole thing. Short quotations cannot convey the excellence of it.

The first act does have more to it than simply the portrayal of the Huxtable menage. We are introduced to Philip and his mother (Mr. Huxtable's sister), and we learn that his father, Constantine Madras, some thirty years ago left England but has now returned to take part in the sale of the Madras House, and possibly of Roberts and Huxtable, to an American financier. And the chief figure in act 2 is spoken of—a Miss Yates, an employee of the firm who is pregnant and refuses to divulge the identity of the father.

We move in act 2 to the offices of Roberts and Huxtable and to episode number two in the theme of the play. This is mainly concerned with Miss Yates, the unfortunate girl who is going to have a baby out of wedlock. Unexpectedly, however, when Philip interviews her she does not consider herself especially unfortunate. She still refuses to name the father of her child or to demand any financial assistance from him. She admits frankly that she knew what she was doing and that she enjoyed it, for a time at least. Philip sympathizes with Miss Yates, as Barker himself appears to, for she has vitality and an appreciation of the value of life. She is an older, less well educated, lower-class Ann Leete, though of course Ann got married; and she is a direct contrast to Amy O'Connell with her cowardly fears about bringing a new life into the world.

This theme of a woman refusing to marry the father of her child was popular with Barker's contemporaries. Hankin, for example, in *The Last of the DeMullins* (1908, before *The Madras House*) and Houghton in *Hindle Wakes* (1912) use it. And in Galsworthy's *The Eldest Son* (written in 1909, produced and published in 1912) Freda refuses to marry her employer's son, although he is the father of her child, because he no longer loves her.

In act 2 of *The Madras House* we are introduced to other women also directly related to the Roberts and Huxtable establishment. Miss Chancellor, who is in charge of the girls, is a sexless old maid whose conventional morality is outraged even more by the indecent attitude of Miss Yates than by her wicked behavior. A third woman involved in the situation is Mrs. Brigstock, wife of an employee who has been caught kissing Miss Yates and who has been suspected of having done more. Mrs. Brigstock angrily demands that her husband's name be publicly cleared. Poor Brigstock has not even dared to admit before that he has been married for four years because of the insecurity he feels in his job and has continued living in at the establishment and seeing his wife surreptitiously for an hour or two at a time. Philip's wife, Jessica, enters the play at this point also. In contrast to Miss Yates, whom she finds an "Ugly little woman," Jessica is a highly refined, well bred lady.

Act 3 takes us to the Madras House itself and presents us with a most entertaining and thoughtful discussion of the place of woman in western civilization. There is a meeting for the purpose of selling the firm, but before the transaction is even mentioned we see a parade of models in the latest French gowns, which are to be copied for production in England, and are shown how great a part sex plays in our lives. Barker has an opportunity here to have a man of a different civilization comment on ours, using the device which the eighteenth century found so convenient for satire. Here, however, it is not a Chinese philosopher or an Indian king who criticizes English manners and morals but an ex-patriate Englishman, Constantine Madras.

Constantine, a handsome, virile man and quite the most fascinating character in the play, is attracted by women. He has left his wife and son, his homeland, and his Christian religion for a harem, Mesopotamia, and Mohammedanism in order to be able to relegate sex to the place in life he believes it should have. He recognizes that women have their purpose—the perpetuation of the race, but in England men are distracted by them, for they parade their attractions everywhere and are not being put to their use in the best way.

Upper-class life, says Constantine, is conducted entirely like a flirtation in a ball room. "Every great public question . . . all politics, all
religion, all economy is being brought down to the level of women's
emotion."[1] This is eating away the strength of men and weakening
the world, without men being aware of what is happening. Women
have good qualities, admits Constantine, but not "morals or intellect
in our sense of the words"; so they should be kept hidden from the
outside world. It would be simpler, Constantine is certain, to allow
polygamy and harems, for women in Europe are prisoners in any case.
Huxtable's six daughters would be happier and Huxtable himself
would find life simpler if he had only to reward one man to marry all of
them. Women in Europe are kept economically. They are imprisoned
in places like the "chaste little fortress" which is the Huxtable home,
or they are prisoners in an "industrial seraglio" like Roberts and
Huxtable, or they are exhibited as models as at the Madras House.
They are failing to perform their one great function—to bear children. To climax his tirade, Constantine holds up a new woman's hat
and exclaims to the men: "A cap of slavery! You are all idolaters of
women . . . and they are the slaves of your idolatry."

These reflections of Constantine's, much of which Philip (and
Barker) seem to relish, are occasioned by the meeting of a group of
men come together to deal in aphrodisiacs, as Philip says. Mr. State,
the American financier, has interested himself in the women's clothing business not because he wants to make money, he explains, but
because he "felt the need of getting into touch with what Goethe
refers to as the woman-spirit . . . drawing us ever upward and on."
He admits that he makes successful use of sexual attraction to promote
sales. In one of his establishments the ladies' department is staffed by
tall, tanned athletes, and in the men's department the "Mean Sensual
Man" is served by beautiful women—"Always of course within the
bounds of delicacy," he adds. Mr. State has become interested in the
"Woman's Movement," which he interprets as woman's self-expres-
sion, primarily through clothes. So he is going to help the middle-
class woman of England attain her birthright to be attractive. But the
shine on this knight's armor reveals itself as the glitter of coin as he
says, "And remember, gentlemen, that the Middle Class Women of
England . . . think of them in bulk . . . they form one of the great-

est Money Spending Machines the world has ever seen."

After this contrast between the sentimental and yet almost indecently practical Mr. State and the exotic and yet also practical Constantine and the civilizations they represent, Philip, always the thoughtful observer, puts the question in Barker's mind to Major Thomas: "Tommy . . . what's the purpose of it all? . . . What do we slow-breeding, civilised people get out of love . . . and the beauty of women . . . and the artistic setting that beauty demands? For which we do pay rather a big price, you know, Tommy. What do we get for it?"

Act 4 brings more light on this query and gives us the author's conclusion—as much as there is one—to the theme of the play. Constantine visits Philip's home and once again meets his forsaken wife. He does not fare so well in this scene, for he is uneasy in her presence, and the unhappiness he has caused her creates sympathy for the woman. Also we discover now that the father of Miss Yates's child is none other than Constantine himself. He feels demeaned by her refusing him any right to his own child. Philip influences our attitude toward his father here by expressing satisfaction that "some woman's been found at last to put you in your place."

Philip blames his father and mother both for his having "grown up inclined to dislike men and despise women" because of the bickering union he is the product of and suggests that his father should pay some attention to the rearing of the children he brings into the world. He grants that his father sent him to a proper school, but asks, "Who taught me that every pretty, helpless woman was a man's prey . . . and how to order my wife out of the room?" Obviously Constantine's attitude toward women is not the ideal in Barker's view despite the fact that Constantine has been given such a wonderful opportunity to chastise England in the preceding act. "Father," says Philip, "don't you realize that . . . in decadent England, at least, this manliness of yours is getting a little out of date . . . that you and your kind begin to look foolish at last?" In any case, Constantine, out of place in his native land, plans to leave once again for Mesopotamia.

It is in this last act that Philip does most of his talking and the relationship between him and Jessica is illustrated. His attitude toward women is quite different from his father's and Major

Thomas's. Companionship is what he wants between a man and a woman. He hates "that farm-yard world of sex." He is not satisfied with the world as it is. "Neither Art nor Religion nor good manners" have made it a desirable place for him. He is refusing State's offer to continue as director of the firm and is going to try to get on the County Council "to do dull, hard work over drains and disinfectants" in order to save his soul. He intends to take his daughter out of her expensive school because she must be taught to know the ugliness in life as well as beauty, culture, and good manners. He explains that giving up beautiful things is not easy for him; it is like yielding his soul to the control of those we tend to scorn at present. "For that's Public Life. That's Democracy. But that's the Future." Women must do this, too; it is the price they pay for freedom.

Jessica says she hates to think about such unpleasant things just as she shuts her eyes to the ugliness of the streets and finds refuge in art. If this willful blindness is to continue, however, insists Philip, "Then there's precious little hope for the Kingdom of Heaven upon earth," and then "good and clever people are costing the world too much. Our brains cost too much if we don't give them freely. Your beauty," he says to Jessica, "costs too much if I only admire it because of the uglier women I see . . . even your virtue may cost too much, my dear. Rags pay for finery and ugliness for beauty, and sin pays for virtue."

Philip then turns in this talk with his wife to the subject of Tommy. Jessica complains that Tommy thinks she wants him to kiss her while she never has that intention. Philip, however, sees through her, and tells her that she only wants him to want to kiss her but never actually to do it. Jessica points out that if she were not cultured and civilized she might not be so virtuous. Philip replies, in a remark that sounds like Candida telling Morell that it is not her virtue that keeps her true to him, "Look here, if it's only your culture keeps you from kissing Tommy . . . kiss him." Jessica calls to his attention the fact that wicked women can become prostitutes and plain women have several possible professions, but she has been brought up only "to be charming and to like dainty clothes."

As is evident, Barker in this discussion is still concerned with the position of women in society. Philip has hope that humanity may be maturing at last. Men and women may be finding happiness and beauty in more serious activities than showing off fashionable clothes and indulging in sex; they may be enjoying moments of calm understanding such as he and Jessica experience at times. (Here occurs one of the few impossible lines of dialogue in the play: Jessica says happily, "Do you mean when we sometimes want to shake hands?") The main idea of the play is seen in Philip's comment: "Male and female created He them . . . and left us to do the rest. Men and women are a long time in the making . . . aren't they?" But that is the goal—men and women, not male and female. He and Jessica agree as the curtain falls that the task will be difficult, but the goal has to be achieved.

It is quite apparent from this account of *The Madras House* that it is almost entirely a play of intellectual conversations, and the objections to it as not being a play can be understood. A contemporary review expressing the attitude of those preferring a well-made play recognizes Barker's ability in characterization and dialogue but complains that this play is "philosophy of life, it is propaganda, it is even conversation and portraiture, but there is no play." A specific objection made is that the play presents the six Huxtable sisters in act 1 only to drop them completely thereafter and end with an entirely different set of characters.[2] Even Shaw's *Misalliance*, a conversational play which is less well unified in its theme than *The Madras House*, has more plot interest. But taking as a definition of drama Barker's own—"anything that can be made effective upon the stage of a theatre by human agency,"[3] we need not argue about whether *The Madras House* be a play, only about its effectiveness.

About the effectiveness of the play there are varying opinions. Most of the adverse criticisms center on its construction and on the weakness of the last act. The first three acts of the play are extremely well done, as a whole and in their details. After Constantine departs the scene, however, and Philip and Jessica are left to their intellectual discussion, the play bogs down. Walter Kerr observes in commenting on the British National Theatre production of it in 1977, "Sobriety doesn't just overtake it; it overwhelms it."[4] This loss of interest comes partly because the characters speak in generalities rather than specifically of themselves,[5] partly because the dialogue is not witty like Shaw's and we are therefore more conscious of being preached at, and partly because of the character of Philip.

So long as Philip remains in the background, more or less, inject-ing a perceptive remark now and then into the conversation, he serves a valuable purpose. But when he is in the foreground he is too colorless to arouse much interest. Of course it is easier to tear down than to construct, easier to draw a fascinating scoundrel or a ridicu-lous fool than to portray equally effectively a sober intellectual. As the elder Voysey is more powerful and intriguing than Edward, so the "character" roles in *The Madras House* hold our attention more readily than the role of Philip. He is described by Barker as having "intellec-tual passion," but still he leaves us cold. Thomas warns him not to think he can improve the nation by "tidying it up." Just this sort of "tidying up" is what people like Philip and Edward Voysey are called upon to do, as Alice tells Edward. Philip has something of Trebell's flaw also of detachment from other people, but he lacks the forceful-ness which gives Trebell power as a politician and as a character in the theater.

When Barker revised the play in 1925, he tightened the dialogue throughout, improved some awkward phrasings, and cut out some of the more ponderous moralizing (as he did also in his revisions of *The Voysey Inheritance* and *Waste*). Yet he still failed to make the last act very effective.

Favorable comments on the play, however, are more numerous than the unfavorable, and better justified. After admitting that it is talky, Ludwig Lewisohn says he believes that no one who can over-come the conventional idea of what a play should be can see this one "without keen intellectual amusement, rich reflection, or that pleas-urable enlargement of experience which makes naturalistic art so permanent and so sustaining."[6] That the play was effective in the theater is attested to by many. Of the New York production in 1921 Robert A. Parker was most enthusiastic, calling it "the most signifi-cant play in New York" and recommending "compulsory attendance by all American playwrights, incipient or confessed. . . . In this play," he says, "Granville Barker has dramatized his own mind. He has made a play of a point of view." Parker is quite right in praising it as "a comedy at which we need not check our intelligence at the door."[7] John van Druten credits the first act of *The Madras House* with showing him that an exciting play could be written around a Sunday morning in a home near the Crystal Palace and thus encouraging him to write, for the only kind of play he felt he could do was one about the kind of people he knew and that was not the sort of play he had seen before Barker's.[8]

The Madras House is not a perfect play, but it is for most of its length very entertaining. Certainly the merciless comic portrayal of the Huxtables is superb, even though their situation no longer exists. The living-in system has been abolished, and Miss Yates's problem is outdated. Nonetheless these details have value as a portrayal of the life of the early twentieth century, and the broader aspects of the question of the position of women in society are still quite relevant. One has only to look at the advertisements in any magazine or on television to see how sex is still being used in our daily lives to sell everything from toothpaste to men's socks.

Barker's careful workmanship is perhaps better illustrated by this play than by any other. The weaving of all of the details, some of which at the time seem insignificant, into the fabric of the whole is not something quickly achieved. The play might also be compared to a carefully wrought symphony: the four movements are separate, but they still make a unified whole.

The naturalistic trend of Barker's work continues in *The Madras House* in the characterization and the dialogue, as Ludwig Lewisohn suggests. He points out that the "curtains" are not those of the well-made play, nor are they even those of the naturalistic plays of Galsworthy or Hauptmann, where at the end of an act some sort of concluding observation notes a stage in the development of the play. Barker carries the naturalistic technique one step further by ending each act in the middle of a conversation, and indeed ending the whole play in the same way. This is not true of acts 1 and 3 so much as of acts 2 and 4, but the curtains are not at all artificially theatrical in any of the acts. The manner in which the events of the play are connected as they often are in life simply by the presence of the same man as a participant in each is also an extension of the naturalistic technique, says Lewisohn.[9] It should be pointed out, however, that naturalistic though the play is in these ways, Barker is not in *The Madras House* primarily concerned with a naturalistic portrayal of life but rather with ideas, and that the presentation is at times exaggerated to the realm of satire, especially with the Huxtables.

The influence of Shaw on Barker is frequently mentioned in connection with *The Madras House* as with others of his plays. True, this is again a play of intellectual discussion with a very loose structure. There is, however, really less discussion here that does not bear directly on the subject than in much of Shaw, and there is again some of Galsworthy's balanced presentation of various sides of the problem. The naturalness of the details suggests Chekhov, and the performances which Barker directed insisted on a natural style of acting. [10] But the emotional quality of Chekhov is missing. Intellectual passion there is, but not emotional warmth.

The Madras House comes, in the chronological listing of his plays, at the midpoint of Barker's career as a dramatist. Original, perceptive, intelligent—these are terms which can be applied to this work as to the earlier ones. Swinnerton's comment on Barker at this point in his development is fully justified: ". . . [*The Madras House*] made one feel that when the author had grown to his full stature he would be fit to paint the whole of English life as no other modern dramatist could do." [11] Unfortunately in his later plays Barker did not expand sufficiently in his accomplishment to fill such a broad canvas.

Rococo

Rococo (written and produced in 1911) [12] is an exception to the majority of the plays of Granville Barker in that it contains much physical action of a most violent kind. It starts with a fight (or rather two sets of hand-to-hand struggle) and ends the same way, with the final act being the smashing of the giant vase about which the fighting has started. This one-act farce is in no way an important contribution to English literary drama, nor does it show any special step forward in the development of Barker as a dramatist. It does serve to illustrate the fact that he did not invariably write intellectual plays.

For theatrical appeal Barker uses in this farce some of the best tried-and-true devices. A comic struggle is almost always a surefire source of laughs. The play begins with the Vicar flat on his back, pinned down by the knee of his nephew-by-marriage. Even more surefire is a fight between two women. The Vicar's old maid sister,

Miss Underwood, is shaking Mrs. Reginald (the nephew's wife) by the elbows from behind. Mrs. Underwood (the Vicar's wife) stands by helpless, anxious about what the servants will think. After a bit, when the struggle has ceased, Mr. Uglow, brother of Mrs. Underwood, is discovered under a table refusing to come out until he has been given his wig, which has somehow fallen off during the melee. A man who is vain about his wig is another unfailing source of laughs, and Barker has Miss Underwood make numerous pointed remarks about it.

Why is the vicarage in such a turmoil? It is all because of a rococo vase which Mrs. Underwood's sister-in-law Jane has left Mrs. Underwood in her will, and which Mr. Uglow demands as rightfully his because Jane's late husband (and his and Mrs. Underwood's brother) had promised it as an heirloom to the family, and men outrank women as members of the family. It is not as if the vase were very valuable or anyone really wanted it. But the old men insist it is the principle of the thing that matters. There is some heated discussion of whom the vase really belongs to, interspersed with Miss Underwood's acid comments on Mr. Uglow's wig.

The characters are sketched in with some degree of detail. Mr. Uglow, for example, is amusing in his insistence on accuracy. He corrects his dead brother's mistake in referring to the vase in his deathbed letter as having been presented to him by the emperor of Germany—"They're German Emperors, not Emperors of Germany," insists Uglow. The brother's letter refers to his "dear wife." "Why he called her his dear wife I don't know," splutters Uglow. "They hated each other like poison."

During the first part of the play the vase itself is not in evidence. Mr. Uglow demands to see it; it has been damaged, he is sure. Miss Underwood finally carries it in. Barker describes it thus: *"It is two feet in height. It is lavishly blotched with gold and white and red. It has curves and crinkles. Its handles are bossy. My God, it is a Vase!"* The argument continues until it leads to physical combat once more, begun as earlier by Miss Underwood boxing Mr. Uglow's ears. Suddenly the participants fall against the table on which the vase stands; the vase is knocked over and crashes to the floor, smashed to pieces. And the play is over.

In this play Barker characteristically satirizes the English middle class; the stage directions, as in *The Madras House*, are as entertaining as the dialogue. The detailed description of the vicarage, for example, filling almost two and one-half pages, emphasizes its middle-class ugliness.

This one-acter is of no historical importance, certainly, but it is hardly the "cracked crock" that one unsympathetic reviewer called it.[13] On the contrary, it is a very funny curtain-raiser.

The Harlequinade

The Harlequinade, written in 1913 in collaboration with Dion Clayton Calthrop and produced in the same year, is a return to somewhat the same tone of fantasy dealing with traditional figures of the theater as is found in the Pierrot play, *Prunella*, by Barker and Housman. Music is used in this play, too, but instead of a pleasantly sentimental love story this work proves to be a dramatized history, in abbreviated form, of the stage itself, presented with some satire on audiences, on theatrical conventions, and on popular types of drama in various centuries. It is also a statement of the authors' faith in what is permanent in the theater—the spirit of make-believe, and of their faith in the theater itself as the home of that spirit. *The Harlequinade* is a short play, divided into five scenes with a surrounding framework and interludes of comment by a sort of chorus consisting of fifteen-year-old Alice, who explains with great pleasure what is taking place, and her Uncle Edward, who restrains her exuberance at times and makes some sly comments of his own. Though published in a volume by itself, it is short enough to have been presented originally as the curtain-raiser for Bernard Shaw's *Androcles and the Lion*.

Alice and Uncle Edward are already seated when the audience begins to arrive, one on either side of the stage in front of a grey and black proscenium, across which blue curtains are hung to hide the stage within the stage on which the various episodes take place. Alice knits or crochets and Uncle Edward reads his paper until it is time for the performance to begin, and they glance up at the audience occasionally to see how many there are and what sort of group it is. The audience need not be large, the authors tell us, but a good audience is one which tries to enjoy the performance. Good-natured remarks are scattered throughout about the spectators and their reactions to the play. Comments are made about their tardiness, the lack of applause, their limited taste in plays, their condescending observations on what they have seen, and their lack of understanding.

In addition to the chorus, there is another element in the play which is incidental to the central material—an element which spoofs philosophy and learning. This involves a Philosopher who has always insisted that there are no gods and who in the very presence of Mercury on the banks of the Styx goes on insisting that he is right. This Philosopher is given the job of ferrying souls across the river while Charon accompanies Mercury to earth for a long weekend lasting several centuries. "A final and a wholesome exercise in what he calls his philosophy," says Mercury, "to row all day from a place he has never understood to a place he doesn't believe in." Mercury borrows the Philosopher's coat and his mask. The coat is covered with patches to suggest poverty, because the only man who needs to be a philosopher is a poor man, and the mask is to hide his face, so that it cannot reveal whether what he said was sensible or not. This is how the Harlequin costume originated, Alice says.

The framework within which the various episodes are placed is the search by Mercury for Psyche (the Soul), who has gone to earth to fulfill her need for human love, explains Alice, but when she tries to return to the gods she cannot unless she discovers a love equal to hers. Then, since the two souls in love exceed the human condition, when their earthly existence ends they grow wings and go to the realm of the gods. This excuse for the play is unimportant, really, and serves only to start off the series of scenes in which the same set of characters appear under different names and different circumstances. On earth Mercury becomes Harlequin, Charon becomes Pantaloon, Momus (Charon's half-brother, who has swum the Styx to join Mercury because he, too, is bored and wants adventure) becomes Clown. Before leaving for earth, Charon and Momus foreshadow the characters they are to become by indulging in a few old jokes and bits of horseplay.

The next scene is a representation of a fifteenth-century Italian pantomime, with Psyche discovered as Columbine. She is married to

Gelsomino, who neglects her for his books because, after all, they are married. He neglects her, that is, until the Man of the World comes along and shows interest in her. Then Harlequin, Pantaloon, and Clown help him play a trick on the Man of the World by disguising him as Columbine. Thus disguised, he keeps her rendezvous with the Man of the World, who goes off in embarrassment, after which the lovers are reunited. This is all performed in delightful pantomime with gleeful commentary by Alice.

The characters next appear in an eighteenth-century English comedy of manners. Harlequin is the valet Quin to the young hero (Lord Eglantine), who is almost nothing more than his image in the mirror, he is so much interested in his clothes (echoes of *Sartor Resartus*). Harlequin has to change this beau into a true man because, Alice explains, "Harlequin is the spirit of man wanting to come to life." Columbine, here called Richardson, is the country girl who has come to work as a chambermaid in the big city. Clown is a friend of the young man, and Pantaloon is his lawyer. Eglantine has been duped by a Woman of the World but learns just in time in order to save the last of his possessions what the true state of affairs is and that he really loves the chambermaid. Ashamed and in despair, he fires a shot at his head, but instead of his falling lifeless to the floor, the mirror shatters into pieces. The real man, the man with a soul, thus emerges when the reflection of wig, snuff, and lace is smashed.

This episode mocks the drama of the eighteenth century, but even more it makes fun of the manners and morals of that time. Quin dresses a wig stand and chair in the clothes of his master; he presents Richardson to it formally, she bows, and the wig stand bows back. When Eglantine enters, Quin removes the lord's cloak, hat, and coat to the accompaniment of a minuet; the lord sits in a chair and looks quite like his wig stand. He has gambled all night and lost, and this is his wedding day, with only two hours in which to dress! He asks for his epigrams on love. But these artificialities seem inappropriate beside the artless song of Richardson, and even Eglantine realizes it. The lord's sense of honor is extreme: Pantaloon reminds him that if he pays his gambling debts and his fiancée's bills, he will be a pauper. "But yet a gentleman who has given his word and not broken it," is Eglantine's reply. When Pantaloon warns him that his fiancée might possibly die or withdraw her consent, so he should at least wait until they are married to settle her debts, Eglantine exclaims: "I will not allow you to cast a doubt either on her perfect health or her perfect honour . . . nor let the shadow of one rest on mine." His shame on learning that he has been duped is happily overcome by true love for the simple and sweet Richardson.

From the artificiality of eighteenth-century England we jump, under the guidance of Alice, to America in the machine age. Harlequin, Columbine, Clown, and Pantaloon have been cast aside by the theater in a machine-oriented world, for drama has become intellectual and the theater is organized along efficient commercial lines. In their bitterness in criticizing the importance of machinery in America and its effect on the theater, the authors put words into the mouth of Alice which an ingenuous fifteen-year-old cannot be expected to have thought of herself.

The episode, however, which follows this attack on the machine age is a clever satire on mechanized entertainment. The curtains part on a backdrop covered with advertisements. The Man of the World here has become the Business Manager, and a very wicked one, complete with silk hat and big cigar. Harlequin and his companions find that the 99th Street Theatre has become "Number 2613 of the five thousand Attraction Houses controlled by the Hustle Trust Circuit of Automatic Drama." They cannot get jobs because there are no actors any more. There is no author of the play because Factories of Automatic Dramaturgy grind out the plays. The president of the circuit has formed an alliance with the cinema and gramophone interests, and after some years of experiment in the scientific production of drama, he has perfected the new medium. Now there are twenty-three factories turning out forty different types of canned plays. The public have to like this stuff, says the Man of the World, for they get nothing else.

He invites the group to watch a rehearsal—one rehearsal is all that is necessary—of "Love: a Disease." The performance is nightmarish. No actors are needed, for two gramophones speak the lines and stage directions are displayed on the wall. Pictures are used only with the less intellectual kinds of drama. In something like this play from the "High Brow Ibsen Series" they only confuse the thought process. The four spectators are horrified. Clown begs Harlequin to try his magic once more, to save the theater and the manager, too. Harlequin thereupon strikes the machines with his wand. They disappear magically, and the Man of the World falls through a trap door in the midst of red fire.

The amount of truth in this fantastic prophecy made in 1913 is amazing. The description of the manufacture of plays for the Hustle Trust sounds very much like the assembly-line production of movies for the masses in the not too distant past of Hollywood and like the present-day duplication of situation comedies and detective dramas for television. Barker and Calthrop were uncomfortably close to accuracy in their prediction.

After this episode Mercury and his companions return to the Styx at the end of the play. They discover the Philosopher now garbed as a member of Parliament. He denies that he is anything so impractical as a philosopher; he is a Political Economist. He writes blue books (that is, government reports) and laws and has founded several rowing academies, though he cannot row and has given the Styx boat to a museum, for he insists still that there is nothing on the other side of the river because that is the verdict of the latest theorists.

Clarence Britten in a contemporary review points out that *The Harlequinade*, intentionally or not, is in the tradition of the burlesque of dramatic styles and technical devices which goes back through Sheridan's *The Critic*, Villiers's *The Rehearsal*, Beaumont and Fletcher's *The Knight of the Burning Pestle*, to Bottom the Weaver in *A Midsummer Night's Dream*.[14] Britten is speaking of the whole play in this comment, but the continuation of this old tradition is actually best illustrated in *The Harlequinade* by the last scene. The style of the fifteenth-century Italian pantomime is not burlesque. It is a romantic presentation of the magic of the theater with a simple emotional appeal. The comedy of manners scene can be considered a burlesque of that type of play, but actually it is more an attack on the fashionable way of life in the eighteenth century in the best tradition of *The Spectator* papers.

Not until the episode depicting the theater of the future with its gramophone stars do we really get fully into the tradition of burlesque. Here we have Harlequin and his friends present at the rehearsal of the play as in Villiers's and Sheridan's classics. But the methods of the older dramatists and of Barker and Calthrop are somewhat different. Instead of merely questions asked and answers given in all seriousness but containing the sting of the satire, the visitors in *The Harlequinade* in addition express directly and forcibly their disapproval of what they hear and see.

The play which is presented in the play within the play within the play in this scene is a burlesque of the intellectual drama. There is no plot, says the Man of the World, only a conversation. The first act consists of a man explaining to a woman how everything bores him. She is at a loss for words. Act 2 is taken up with his wanting her advice about marriage. She again has no answer. These acts we only hear about from the Man of the World; we do not see them. But act 3, of which we see a portion until the whole thing becomes too much for the visitors, contains the action, such as it is. The Man of the World gives a résumé of it: "About half way through he moves across to her and says: 'Don't cry, little girl, I can always shoot myself!' And then he finds out that she is stone deaf from birth, and hasn't really heard a word he said. So she goes forth into the world to learn the Oral system, while he awaits her return, when he will begin again." This perhaps cannot be called a fair commentary on the plays of Shaw or of Barker himself (though apparently he had sense of humor enough to laugh even at himself here), but it does suggest the direction in which the plotless, conversational drama of the day might at its worst proceed.

The Harlequinade actually has three levels of meaning. First there is the story of the gods who come to earth, appear in various guises, and then go back home. Then there is the history, partly satiric, of types of drama and methods of presentation in various centuries. Finally there is the level of the deepest meaning—that of the criticism of life and of the position of the actor and the theater itself in various periods of history. To judge by this play, life in fifteenth-century Italy was simple. The actors were given an opportunity to perform their magic and appeal to the emotions. In eighteenth-century England the magic had been lost somewhat, and the actor's social position was lower: Columbine is a maid and Harlequin a valet. Life was artificial and superficial, as we see in the Lord Eglantine situation. In the look into the future the gods are completely out of the theatrical picture. It has become the machine age, and the intellectual drama has flung out the simple charms and emotions of Harlequin, Columbine, Clown, and Pantaloon. But not for ever or really, says Alice. We cannot do without them, "For the seed of the gods is sown in the hearts of men. The seeds of Love and of the Magic of High Adventure and of Laughter and of Foolishness, too."

Here is the real meaning of this play. These are the things which we must have for life to be real and worthwhile, and it is in the theater that we can find them and believe in them. We recall what Alice has said early in the play about things disappearing that we stop believing in, and about our believing the make-believe more than the real: "But Mercury knew that if people won't believe a thing when you say it's real, they'll just as good believe it and understand it a great deal better when it only seems make-believe. And that's Art." It is in this spirit of make-believe, Barker and Calthrop say in their foreword, that the play is presented. But in the guise of make-believe is something very real and important which people should be made to understand.

Some reviewers were not much impressed with *The Harlequinade*. One called it "barren work," with no sign of "creative energy or vision."[15] Another chided Barker for trying "to deal with the gods, and the childlike spirit, and feeling, and imagination and vision—all the big things of the golden age," when these are not within the scope of his ability.[16]

Barker was bothered enough by these comments to write a reply as a letter to the editor in which he politely indicates that *The Harlequinade* is a parable but that it is primarily intended to be entertainment. He incidentally also states that he does not approve of attempts to fathom the secrets of collaboration. He admits that the "bad aesthetics" of the play are his[17]—whatever he meant by that term; it probably includes the ideas about the art of the theater and the relationship of that art to life, for Barker in his critical works, too, expresses a similar belief in the power of the drama as a teacher. The interest in the traditional Harlequin-Columbine story may have been Calthrop's contribution. He later published a brief account of Punch and Judy in Europe which reveals a similar interest.[18]

One may criticize the play as rambling. One may argue that the symbolism or allegory, perhaps because of the attempt to fit together portions of the play which do not go together very well, is sometimes obscure and inconsistent and is best thought of only in a general sense of the gods turned actors to try to liberate the spirit of man. But, on the other hand, the play is entertaining. Robert Benchley said of its production in New York in 1921: "Speaking not as a professional play-goer, but as a rather sentimental old thing . . . , we may say that 'The Harlequinade' gave us a great deal of pleasure." He adds that it is not actually at all sentimental. [19] Moreover, the play has good criticism of life and of the theater, and despite the fact that Barker was accused of not seeing the gods at all, he and Calthrop certainly in this play see the godlike spirit of human beings which can be stirred and exalted by the unlimited magic of the theater. And they succeed in this play in creating a great deal of that magic.

Vote by Ballot

Vote by Ballot (written in 1914, produced in 1917) is a thoughtful comedy in one act. Its concern with the English middle class (upper-middle here, Barker points out) and with English politics is typical of the author, and so is its revelation of the fact that our inner lives are often kept secret from even our closest intimates.

The characters are Mr. and Mrs. Torpenhouse, Lord Silverwell (recently elevated), and his son Noel. Noel has just lost the election for the House of Commons by one vote and so has lost the seat which his father had held for thirty years and which the father had promised the Liberal party leaders would be safe when they offered to put him in the House of Lords. Torpenhouse has all these years been committee chairman for Silverwell as well as manager of his shoe manufacturing business. When Noel refuses to run again, they all feel that Torpenhouse should be the next candidate. But Torpenhouse suddenly confesses that this is his hour of victory, for he voted against Noel and, even more surprising, he has been a Tory all along.

Silverwell is amazed. This is something he has never dreamed of. For all these years Torpenhouse has submerged himself in Silverwell's affairs. It is his ability that has made the business so successful. It is he who is responsible for Silverwell becoming a successful Liberal poli-

tician—Liberal because he did not think he could make Silverwell
into a Tory, which required qualities of strength and brains lacking in
Silverwell. In these ways he has been completely true to his employer,
but his private beliefs he has reserved to himself. Not even his wife has
known. In fact, he has told her that she must not ever wish to
understand everything about him, a situation she has become rec-
onciled to. Now, however, she decides that she will henceforth use
her ballot but keep her vote a secret.

Lord Silverwell feels that somebody should be told of this decep-
tion, for the whole situation impresses him as somewhat immoral,
especially Torpenhouse's offer to stay on as chairman for a while
longer. Torpenhouse will have no public revelations, however. "Is the
ballot secret . . . or is it not?" Besides, how honest is Silverwell
himself? He advertises the boots he makes as being the best, and yet
he does not wear them himself nor does his son.

Then, to justify his behavior, Torpenhouse explains how his decep-
tion started. He felt indebted to Silverwell in the early days and
wanted to help him. He was sure it would not do the country any
harm to add one more like Silverwell to hundreds already talking in
Parliament, and it has not. Yet in this way Torpenhouse became a
hypocrite. Silverwell in his direct and simple fashion demands to
know if he has ever asked Torpenhouse to do anything crooked for
him. But life is not so easy as that, morality is not so clear-cut, replies
Torpenhouse, with a touch of the basic philosophy of *The Voysey
Inheritance*. Ironically, Silverwell has been changing to the Tory view
for somé years now (this is one reason he has been elevated to the
peerage), suggests Torpenhouse, and this has salved his conscience a
little.

Not sure whether he is angry or not, Silverwell takes his leave.
Noel admires Torpenhouse, and Mrs. Torpenhouse is understanding.
Torpenhouse himself is worn out from all the excitement. He would
like to go to Spain to live for a while, by himself since Mrs. Torpenhouse probably would not want to—that is, if Silverwell will allow
him to resign from the shoe firm. Just now, however, he goes up to his
room to sleep.

Thus in typical naturalistic style we do not know how the situation will eventually work out, but we have seen the effective presentation of a serious moral question and satire on English politics.

Farewell to the Theatre

Farewell to the Theatre (written in 1916), the least dramatic of Barker's three one-act plays, has never been done on the stage, but from the point of view of the author's personal development it is very significant and revealing. In *The Harlequinade* Barker and Calthrop expressed their belief that commercial and mechanical forces in our contemporary life were ruining the theater as a cathedral of the spirit. In *Farewell to the Theatre* we have a more direct and personal expression of this same idea.

The play is in the form of a dialogue between Dorothy Taverner, an aging actress of fifty-three, and her lifelong friend and admirer, a lawyer named Edward. Barker himself refers to it in the opening stage directions as a "talk," and that is all it is. There is no action, but there is revelation of character and ideas. Although Edward has proposed to Dorothy several times through the years, she has always refused to marry him (or anyone else of her admirers); yet she finds him sympathetic enough to expose her innermost thoughts to him. Their dialogue shows a contrast between the materialistic commercial world represented by Edward and the spiritual world of art represented by Dorothy.

Dorothy is producing another play, and Edward has asked to talk with her to convince her that it ought to be her last since she cannot afford to lose any more money if she is to have an income for her old age. She stands to lose money with her plays, for she admits her performances are thought to have deteriorated and her plays are no longer popular. During her sixteen years in management Dorothy has paid some financial dividends—to those who invested money in order to make some, notes Edward, while those who were interested in art and in Dorothy never got any monetary returns. But Dorothy cites her achievement "for Dear Art's sake." It is an impressive one, and strongly reminiscent of Barker's own record, including productions of Shakespeare, Ibsen, Shaw, Galsworthy, Chekhov, Yeats, and Masefield. Those who have given money to her, Dorothy says, have done so for the sake of their souls.

Now, however, Dorothy thinks of herself as already dead, killed by her public. She has been dead since the time of her first failure, which was not an artistic failure in her own eyes; indeed it was the result of her discovery of truth, but the public was not willing to accept truth. She had up to then rehearsed her parts in front of mirrors. The character in whom she first found truth she found not in her own mirrored reflection but in a woman who sewed for her. The public, however, would not pay to see the play, so in the ordinary commercial sense it was a failure. Yet Dorothy knew that she had found freedom from "emptiness of self," and she has never rehearsed in front of mirrors again. (Dorothy here is somewhat like the sixteenth-century beau in *The Harlequinade*, who finds himself when his reflection in the mirror is shattered.) Dorothy has gone on producing plays and acting, not catering to the public which would make her plays financially successful, but being true to her love of knowledge and beauty for their own sake. She has not succumbed to the temptations of the life of comfort which she might have had by marrying Edward because she has discovered what is in the essential sense real.

Barker suggests in *The Harlequinade* that the world of make-believe may be more real than the actual world; in much the same way he has Dorothy say that she as an actress has lived a hundred lives and that she has felt that sometimes actors playing parts, "but with real faith in their unreal," live those lives more truly than real people. But it is not real, protests Edward, and perhaps neither is the next world as they imagine it. Dorothy is nonetheless sure of her faith. Here are two classes of people, then—the artists in their world of make-believe, and the practical materialists in their world of actuality and money. It is easy to see which Barker prefers.

Dorothy is now ready—after this one last play—to withdraw to an abbey she has bought, a place built "to the glory of God," where she has heard a voice within her speak, and where it will speak again. The voice will tell her that the artist gladly gives his soul to the unborn, gladly returns to the nothingness he has always been, for "the world of other people is the only world there is."

Then Dorothy interrupts her reverie to invite Edward to take her to lunch, and as the curtain falls, they enter the real world once again.

The last part of this play is one of the most beautiful and moving scenes in all of Barker's works. He sympathizes with Dorothy so deeply that it seems evident that she is expressing his own attitude toward his life's work in the theater. Things have not gone as he has wished; there is disappointment in that. When Dorothy complains that her public have not appreciated her when she has done her best work, we may with reason think we hear Barker speaking of his own experience. Yet he has done his best; he has been true to his art and this, not financial or popular success, is what counts. There is a tone of sadness here in the criticism of the attitude of the public toward the sort of theater that Barker wants, but there is none of the bitterness of the satire of *The Harlequinade*. It is as if the war years have mellowed Barker, though they have also taken away some of his energy and strength to work actively in his sort of theater. Yet he still believes in his art.

One should not press too far this sort of interpretation of the dramatist's work in relation to his own life, for after all Dorothy is a consistent and convincing character in her own right and not just a mouthpiece for her author's personal grievances. It is significant, however, to note that Barker wrote only two original plays after this one—*The Secret Life* (published in 1923) and *His Majesty* (published in 1928), neither of which has been produced. He no longer acted and took part in producing only on infrequent and special occasions. He did work on translations and adaptations of foreign plays and wrote criticism of value, so his connections with the drama were not entirely severed. But after his marriage to Helen Huntington he no longer depended on the theater for an income and no longer made his home in London. Thus in a very real sense Dorothy Taverner's farewell to the theater is at the same time the farewell of Granville Barker.

Chapter Six

Two Idealists: *The Secret Life* and *His Majesty*

Granville Barker's last two plays were written after World War I. Both *The Secret Life* and *His Majesty* deal with politics, one in democratic England and the other in the hypothetical kingdom of Carpathia. The hero of the first is a disillusioned idealist once prominent in politics but for many years inactive, who is persuaded once again to run for election. The hero of the second is an idealistic king in exile from his country which is in political turmoil, who returns in an attempt to avoid bloodshed. Neither of these plays has been professionally produced. Perhaps, as Margery Morgan suggests, Barker wrote them for the National Theatre whose establishment he always looked forward to but did not live to see, and withheld them from production under other circumstances.[1] Similar to Barker's other plays in their intellectual appeal, they are not likely candidates for popular success in the commercial theater.

The Secret Life

The Secret Life (written 1919—1922) was Granville Barker's first full-length play written after World War I, and his first full-length play since *The Madras House* (1909). The disillusionment and sadness of tone which are apparent in the one-act *Farewell to the Theatre* are evident here also; and the secret inner life which one cannot explain or reveal or perhaps even understand oneself—the inner life in which Trebell felt the loss of his unborn child so painfully that he took his own life, the inner life which Dorothy Taverner wanted to keep inviolate by not marrying Edward—this inner life inexplicably keeps Joan Westbury from marrying Evan Strowde, even though she has been in love with him for eighteen years.

The Secret Life is a strange and difficult play. It is concerned, as one might expect, with characters and ideas rather than action. The play is not lacking in incident; it has almost enough, indeed, as one critic says, "to fit out half a dozen melodramas."[2] It is not a melodrama, however, but a serious psychological study of disillusionment, which is illustrated and contrasted in various well-drawn characters. Barker seems almost uninterested in the physical action, and his hero and heroine are equally detached from the life going on about them.

The plot deals with the love of Evan Strowde for Joan Westbury, and with Evan's political life. Evan is an idealist so disillusioned by contact with the tarnished world that he has withdrawn from active affairs and devotes his time to the writing of a history. Once an important political figure, he is during the course of the play wooed into running for office again, but is not certain that he wants it any more. He lost interest when Joan refused to marry him eighteen years ago, and the war has also left him disillusioned and detached from life. In the first act Joan confesses to Evan that she still, in her innermost self, loves him, though some power within has always kept her from him. She tries to explain her feeling thus: "Perhaps, Evan . . . for the last meaning . . . to love is to love the unattainable." Detached and philosophical though Evan is, he is human enough to remind Joan that she has had a husband and two sons, even though both her sons were killed in the war, whereas he has only his sister Eleanor and the history he has been writing for some years. Joan tries to stir him out of his mood of hopelessness and disbelief, but he admits he has no ambition left in him; he no longer wants to be a political power, though possibly if he could be in love again, he might. He has learned to believe in the unattainable, and nothing else can inspire him. The war has had an influence on him, too. His idealistic beliefs are gone. He has nothing left.

Joan Westbury, too, is a study in disillusion. Almost without feeling since the death of her two sons, she has recently returned from Egypt, where her husband is still in government work. Her house in England has just burned with all her possessions, and she is staying with Evan and his sister. She looks at the moon in the first scene and comments: "And she's dead, poor thing." The burnt house and dead moon are like Joan herself, as she recognizes. Then one more tragedy hits Joan at the end of act 1—her husband dies suddenly in Cairo. In act 2 it seems as if, now that Joan is widowed, she and Evan are finally to be married. But when Evan asks her, she refuses him. Though she still loves him, she says that she cannot marry him, for she has nothing to bring to him. Instead she goes to America with Mr. Kittredge, an elderly American who, with his granddaughter Susan, has been visiting England. Susan stays behind to study English politics.

The disillusion of the younger generation is exemplified in Oliver Gauntlett, the illegitimate son of Evan and Lady Peckham. Evan reenters politics from a desire to help Oliver as much as anything else. Oliver has not been told that Evan is his father, but he has suspected it. Though Oliver has lost an arm in the war, his climbing up a trellis in act 2 to the second story despite his handicap is indicative of the lack of importance of his physical debilitation.[3] It is his loss of faith which is more significant. Mentally unsettled, he has lost his job as a result of his arrest at an anarchist meeting. His only purpose in life now is to destroy. He sees no value in the world and believes that what is needed is a real war that will do a thorough job of destruction so that we can start afresh. Like Joan, he is dead inside. Oliver tells Joan that he loves her, too, but later he seems to be interested in Susan Kittredge and she in him. Oliver's mother thinks that Evan could do some good for Oliver, and Evan takes him on as his secretary for this purpose. Oliver himself wants to work with Evan to try to find out, he says, where Evan has failed in his attempt to get to the essence of things. Oliver is in his disillusioned idealism like Evan himself, and his love for Joan is the same sort of love of the unattainable as is his father's.

Gradually the hatred Oliver said he felt for Evan because he was a failure is dispelled, and in act 2 he quietly tells Evan he knows they are father and son. His pessimistic attitude alters to a more hopeful one. Evan, however, still is without illusions, even harder of heart now that he has returned to politics. He tells Oliver that the surest way to destroy is to fulfill. He has discovered that his vision of the world was nothing like the reality, but just a vision. This realization places one beyond pain and hope, and gives one power. He urges Oliver to learn from him how to replace him. Oliver's comment on this philosophy is simply, "Wouldn't you sooner I killed you now where you sit?"

Although the play creates the atmosphere of disillusion after World War I in not only these three leading characters but in others as well, it is not depressing in its effect. It has a message of hope and faith despite the fact that this hope and faith are for some of the characters hard to find and to maintain. Eleanor Strowde, for example, has never lost her staunch idealism, and when she finds her brother waxing ironical and pessimistic about his ideals, she says that she no longer knows him and that she can help him no longer in his work. When Evan refers to the alarming prospects of the breaking up of the atom, Eleanor gives a reply which shows her confidence in the future: "If we can break it up we can teach it how to behave . . . if we choose."

There is hope, too, in the fact that Joan Westbury finds out her mistake in trying to keep her secret life to herself, in refusing to love and give of her real self ever to another person—even though she does not make the discovery until her dying days. In a moving scene in act 3 she confesses to the understanding old Mr. Kittredge that her sin has been her failure to give her heart, desperately though she has tried and though she has allowed herself to be loved. She has kept her secret self apart from life, and she has failed the man who loved her. Now Joan is dying. Her headaches turn out to have been caused by a tumor on the brain. When news of Joan's illness reaches Evan, he abandons the election without a moment's hesitation and leaves for America, though there is no chance of his seeing Joan alive again.

Susan, the granddaughter of Mr. Kittredge, has a strong faith in life and in the need for trying to do one's part in making ideals into actuality. She insists that Oliver inform Evan of Joan's death—he can still return from Cherbourg for the election. Oliver is sure that Evan will not come back, for he was happy to leave. Susan is equally sure that he will, and that he will be a changed man. She says: "Loving her so to the last . . . and being cheated . . . is like dying for love. He'll be born again . . . in a way." Oliver calls her "Simple Susan!" and accuses her of believing in miracles. She admits that she does, in miracles of that sort, and asks: "Wouldn't you want to be raised from the dead?" When he replies, "No, indeed," she says, "You'll have to be . . . somehow."

In a fashion, as the play progresses, Oliver becomes Evan and Susan becomes Joan. Oliver, even before knowing that he is Evan's son, has still always felt a kinship to him. They are much alike. Susan and Joan, on Joan's departure for America, have agreed to exchange places in a kind of game, as Susan explains. Joan has taken Susan's rooms at home and signs her letters Susan. Susan has not been able to answer them in the same effective manner, but she has been doing and is to do with Oliver the work that Joan failed to do with Evan—the work of encouragement and uplift in the face of temptations toward despair and bitterness. In a play full of symbolic subtlety this exchange of names and location must be significant. Moreover, it is not only England that Barker is portraying in *The Secret Life*, but America, too, and it is from America that spiritual help must come for England. Joan recognizes that the "blasphemous towers of Babel" which are New York are not like Mr. Kittredge, and that he and America will conquer the "monster world" that they represent.

Thus the pessimism of the play is tempered. Joan has learned her tragic mistake about life and holds out hope for the new world, Mr. Kittredge has faith despite everything, Evan may be reborn, Oliver is possibly going to be influenced by Susan, and Susan herself speaks for the future and for faith.

Frequently here as in Barker's earlier plays it is not easy to see what is really his own attitude because of his method of presenting many different points of view and balancing them against each other. But it seems likely that the dialogue between Mr. Kittredge, a writer and a philosopher himself, and Joan in the last moments of her life contains Barker's own beliefs. Things are not clear to us, Mr. Kittredge says; life is difficult; despair and bitterness are easy. Joan replies: "I've tried to be bitter. So have you. And that's a failure." Then the wise and understanding Mr. Kittredge suggests that death marks the end of what this life corrupts. "But, freed from self's claim upon it, scattered, dissolved, transformed, that inmost thing we were so impotently may but begin, new breathed, the better to be. For comfort's sake we lead our busy lives. Who wouldn't want to forget sometimes this strange, new, useless burden of the soul? Left comfortless, we must bear it for a while as bravely as we may."

Melodramatic though the incidents in *The Secret Life* may be in themselves, they are treated in a most unmelodramatic fashion. The whole play is written in a very low key, quiet and thoughtful, with no theatrical curtains or big emotional scenes. The dialogue is naturalistic, and the scenes end not with a punch line or tableau effect, but with the suggestion of life continuing after the curtain. The revelation that Oliver is Evan's son is made almost incidentally and casually rather than with elaborate preparation for it, and Oliver's statement to Evan that he knows of their true relationship is handled with great restraint. In fact, there is such restraint in the face of emotional crises that it may at times, however true it may be to the British character, make the dialogue seem wooden and unconvincing.

In various passages in *The Secret Life* there are echoes of ideas found in Barker's earlier plays. The problem of absolute values which appears prominently in *The Voysey Inheritance* is suggested when the Jewish politician Salomons accuses the English of believing in absolute values. A bit later he advocates what idealistic Philip Madras has found wrong with his civilization—the development at the expense of others of ladies and gentlemen of taste who appreciate the "finer things of life" and turn their backs on ugliness and suffering. Serocold, another politician, finds in idealistic Eleanor "intellectual passion," which is "chilling but admirable" and which Philip Madras has in abundance, too. Reminiscent of Barker's earlier criticism in *The Voysey Inheritance* and *Waste* of the middle-class system of bringing up children is Mr. Kittredge's comment that it is sadistic to teach children ideals that the world does not live by.

The practice found in *The Madras House* of introducing characters and then dropping them in favor of new ones is followed to a degree in *The Secret Life* also. Salomons is well characterized in act 1, scene 1, but he never reappears. Lord Clumbermere, though he is spoken of throughout, does not arrive in person until the last scene of the last act. This method does not, however, reflect a lack of organization in the play. Salomons is an example of disillusioned man; he thinks he knows how to get idealists to sell their principles, though not for money. Thus he fits in with the general picture of disillusion in the first act. Clumbermere, on the other hand, is a manufacturer who combines practicality with idealism. Doing good results in profits, he believes. By manufacturing ink he considers that he is contributing something to poetry and to government. In the expression of ideas like these, Clumbermere helps to create the mood of hope and courage at the end of the play. It is not just by chance that these two characters are introduced into the play when they are.

In its relative obscurity and in the fact that Joan cannot explain fully why she refuses to marry Evan as Ann Leete cannot explain why she proposes to Abud, *The Secret Life* is suggestive of *The Marrying of Ann Leete*. The beginnings of the two plays are similar, too. In *Ann Leete* voices are heard speaking in the dark, and the stage only gradually lightens with the dawn. In *The Secret Life* the first act setting is the loggia of a house near the sea. The loggia is bordered by a stone wall, so that the characters there (who are singing excerpts from *Tristan and Isolde* and talking) cannot be seen unless they stand up. It is night, and the only person in evidence is Joan Westbury, sitting alone on the steps leading down from the loggia. One by one the others stand up or walk across the stage for some reason and thus are gradually revealed to the audience. In this way Barker emphasizes Joan's aloneness from the very beginning.

Some similarities exist, then, between *The Secret Life* and Barker's earlier works. But in a very important sense this play is a departure from the realistic-naturalistic method of *The Voysey Inheritance, Waste,* and *The Madras House*. It goes beyond specific details of financial chicanery, political problems, and the woman question, to broader philosophical questions of practicality versus idealism, of life and death. Here we have a spirituality and a spaciousness that have not appeared so prominently before. In its spirituality it is an extension of the style and mood of *Farewell to the Theatre.* Its spaciousness in subject matter and its technique suggest that Barker, like Chekhov (in *The Cherry Orchard*, for example, in the mysterious sound of the breaking harp string) and like the later Ibsen, is trying to go beyond the conventional physical limitations of the stage.[4] The fact that not only England but America is part of the scene and that France and Egypt are frequently referred to contribute to this feeling of spaciousness, as well as the deep spiritual quality of the subject and the symbolic suggestion of some of the dialogue. Though there is a surface realism in the dialogue, this is not what Barker is most concerned with, but with spiritual reality. The references to the moon and to other lands on this planet expand the locale outwardly. The references to the past and to the future after death expand it in time. The references to the deep inner lives of the characters expand it in the direction of the spirit.

The stage itself is hardly big enough to contain all that is transpiring. The actual physical settings are small, but there is always a suggestion of a greater expanse just beyond them. Though the loggia in act 1 is cramped, it faces the sea and the sky, and we find Joan looking up at the moon. We see only a corner of a long gallery on the second floor in act 2, but action goes on on the terrace outside and below it, and voices are heard speaking outside and even exchanging remarks with the persons on the stage. At one point in act 2, scene 3 Eleanor and Evan discuss politics in the gallery corner while four other characters are playing a game of rounders outside and discussing its rules. Evan, on stage, interrupts his talk with Eleanor to take part for a bit in the outside chatter. Barker also uses the device of having the onstage characters see others approaching the corner of the gallery before they are visible to the audience, and this preparation for their entrance helps expand the actually limited stage area. In all these ways, then, Barker is going beyond the physical limitations of the confined stage set itself to create a feeling of a larger area. It is almost a Shakespearean spaciousness that we find in *The Secret Life*, a quality that Sutton describes in this way: "The play's thought transcends its utterance even as its scenes transcend the stage whereon they are set; for its narrow galleries debouch on paths that circle the world, and its casements open on to infinity."[5]

In its symbolism and its recognition of the mystical nature of life this play perhaps suggests the influence of Maeterlinck on Barker. That there may well have been such an influence is indicated by the fact that Barker wrote an introduction to a volume of three plays of Maeterlinck (*Alladine and Palomides, Interior,* and *The Death of Tintagiles*) which was published in 1911 in which he recognizes the value of symbolism—"the only way of saying much in little."[6] At any rate, about 1920 a change from realism-naturalism in dramatic style was becoming apparent in England. For example, Shaw's *Heartbreak House* (1918), *Back to Methuselah* (1921), and *Saint Joan* (1923) all show the note of fantasy. It is not only in form but in the substance of the plays that this change is evident, a change from an emphasis on man as a creature in society to an expression of a philosophical concern.[7] This change toward a more philosophical drama is clearly seen in *The Secret Life*.

Unquestionably *The Secret Life* is not an easy play to read. The difficulty of understanding it practically every critic has commented on. Edward Shanks, who acknowledges that he was puzzled by Barker's *Ann Leete* and even by *Waste*, says he finds himself "genuinely and honestly puzzled by the drift of his thought in *The Secret Life*." W. A. Darlington made of it "neither head nor tail," and says "that the reasons for the sayings and doings of the characters were utterly enigmatic." Both of these men admit that the obscurity in the play is dispelled by a second reading, but they question whether it could be successfully done on the stage. Darlington says it is "devoid of the fundamental stage virtue of clarity."[8] Shanks frankly admits that did he not know who Barker was, he would conclude that "he was a man of great literary gifts who . . . had better give up all idea of writing for the theatre since he obviously had no understanding of its conditions and its limitations."[9]

When William Archer complained in a letter to Barker that the play was not clear enough for an audience to understand, Barker replied: "I protest I never have—I cannot—write an unactable play; it would be against nature, against second nature anyhow: I act it as I write it. But there is no English company of actors so trained to interpret thought and the less crude emotions, nor as a consequence—any selected audience interested in watching and listening to such things. But that, believe me, human fallibility apart,—mine to begin with—is the extent of the difficulty."[10] One may agree with the critics who pointed out that to get the full significance of the many ideas and subtleties in the play an audience would have to be very acute and intelligent, but at the same time one can recognize that hearing actors speak the lines with the proper emphases and nuances would do much to clear up apparent obscurities. Simply the physical presence of the actors would help distinguish the several individuals who speak in quick succession and alternation in some scenes in the play.

In *The Secret Life*, then, we have a further development by Barker of the possibilities of the stage in its brilliant psychological portrayal of character, its effective presentation of an epoch in English history, and its beautiful expression of philosophical ideas. Difficult though it may be at first reading, this is a play worthy of close attention because of its excellence in conception and execution.

His Majesty

Granville Barker's last original play is *His Majesty* (written 1923 — 1928), a study of revolution in the mythical kingdom of Carpathia after World War I and of an exiled king's return to his country in order to try to stop the bloodshed. The play's interest lies, as usual with Barker, not in the plot, but in the ideas and characters, which are, again as usual, well presented. This work is not difficult to follow, except perhaps in the multitude of characters—there are twenty-one. If *Waste* can be adversely criticized, as it was by some, because it deals with a hypothetical political situation and one therefore that the audience (or reader) is not interested in, then *His Majesty* might be objected to because it deals not only with a hypothetical political situation but with a hypothetical country as well. The fate of an exiled ruler, however, is not one which has no basis in reality, as events both before and after the writing of this play illustrate.

The problem which King Henry XIII of Carpathia faces in this play is not only the problem of an exiled monarch who returns to his country in the midst of a revolution, but more basically that of an idealist in a world of violence, hypocrisy, and disillusion. For Henry is an idealist at the same time as he is a realist about his own position in the world. Having left his country because his people, blaming him for the country's being on the losing side in the war, were apparently anxious to get rid of him (they bombed his grandfather's statue, for example) and because he felt it was the sensible thing to do "to give the Democrats their chance," he is not very desirous of going "back to that puppet show!" He would rather stay in Zurich and take care of his chickens. With the country as unsettled as it is, it would be doubly pleasant to stay away from any responsible position in it.

At this particular time in Carpathia a young man whom the king

has known all his life, Stephen Czernyak, with five thousand followers, is threatening the government of Dr. Madrassy. Henry decides
that he must do his duty and return to try to stop bloodshed and put
his country back into order. The queen is overjoyed because she thinks
he means to fight for his throne, but he actually intends only to
prevent civil war. Returning to Carpathia in act 2, Henry meets with
Madrassy, and by act 3 he manages to arrange an armistice between
Madrassy and Czernyak.

Once back, however, Henry is not sure that he wants to leave
again. He has promised Madrassy to leave once the trouble was ended
if he found that he himself was not wanted in his former kingdom.
Now he is not certain of what he ought to do because he has enjoyed
his position and felt he was popular. He recognizes as his only gift the
ability to get along with his fellowman, which he can do because he
likes him. He believes that there is a place for a king, that the ordinary
man needs someone who is not out to get anything from him, "not
even his vote." Madrassy, however, insists that Henry abdicate or he
will be kept prisoner.

This threat of force irritates the king and he is almost tempted to
stay and fight, but when his followers disobey orders and start firing
on the town they have been staying in, he is ready to surrender. Before
the fighting spreads, however, another politician, Bruckner, who
wants to control the country, has Czernyak killed (in act 4) and then
offers to form an alliance with Henry against Madrassy, recognizing
that Henry's popularity and position as king would be to his advantage. Henry, however, now decides to abdicate, for he dislikes
bargains of this sort and because he has accomplished his purpose of
stopping the civil war. He is willing to accept Britain's offer of haven
in Bermuda and almost lightheartedly faces his future in exile with his
family and his chickens.

Barker's portrayal of Henry is that of a very human king. The
down-to-earth touches of the king's interest in poultry farming and in
his horse (which always went sideways and put Henry in an awkward
position when reviewing the troops), his simplicity (he speaks to
correspondents, and he writes to Czernyak in the first person because
in the formal style his grammar always becomes muddled), his kindness to his loyal if not very bright wife, his ability to accept the truth

about his outdated position ("Europe must face democracy," he says)—all of these details make him a likable human being. His acceptance of his responsibilities, his loyalty to his friends, and his sense of honor make him admirable as well. Like most of Barker's heroes, he is an idealist and one who analyzes his own reactions. Like Edward Voysey, Henry Trebell, Philip Madras, and Evan Strowde, he has a sense of detachment from the hustle and bustle of the materialistic world of affairs; but, unlike them, he is not an intellectual who talks at great length about what must be done to improve society. Thus he is more convincing as a human being. Strange that in his portrayal of a king, Barker has depicted in many ways his most likable and human hero.

Queen Rosamund, too, is a very understandable and convincing character. She is not so clever as Henry—in fact, at times she is almost stupid in her refusal to accept her status as an exiled queen. She insists on proper court etiquette even in Zurich. She is pleased by the fact that the American correspondent correctly bows three times on leaving her presence. She has poor Colonel Guastalla changing time after time from civilian clothes, which he must wear on the streets of Zurich, to his uniform, which he wears indoors only. She would bribe men in Carpathia with the old currency which carries Henry's picture and is now worthless. She tries to conspire against her husband's wishes and without his knowledge to have him reinstated. Foolish though she be, Rosamund is, however, thoroughly likable. Moreover, she is admirable, too, in her kindness and loyalty to her friends, her graciousness, her courage in accompanying Henry back to Carpathia, her willingness to endure hardships, and her steadfastness in what she believes to be right. Henry recognizes her true worth, for when she accuses him of thinking her a fool, he replies that her instinct is often a better guide than his reason.

Barker's understanding of human nature is revealed in numerous little touches in the portrayal of the characters. The queen, for example, has brought with her to Carpathia two Grand Crosses of St. Anne and five Second Class St. Andrews, thinking they may be useful. When she and Henry are about to leave the country at the end, old farmer Jakab comes to bid her farewell and, at his wife's suggestion, to ask her for an order. She tells him that the king has abdicated and can no longer confer decorations, but when she sees his disappointment, she presents him with a medal, saying: "Mr. Jakab! Yesterday you would have been a knight of St. Andrew." Jakab replies: "Now that's most ladylike of your Majesty . . . and I'm much obliged . . . and so'll my wife be. Of course if it's not valid it don't do you any good. But you mean it kindly. Much obliged to your Majesty, I'm sure." This incident, coming on top of the fact that the king has gone to inspect his escort in a quickly procured ready-made suit (having abdicated, he no longer wears his uniform) and followed immediately by the realization that she has no money to pay for a hatbox which has arrived, is too much for Rosamund, and she finally for the first time breaks down and weeps. The queen is bitter about having to leave her country, though she regrets nothing and feels that her experiences have not changed her at all. She thinks she has no work left for her, for all she can do is be queen. Yet when Henry calls her attention to a flattering statement about her in the newspaper account of the interview granted the American correspondent at the beginning of the play, she shows that she is first of all a human being. She becomes immersed in the paper as the train takes them to the frontier.

The interest of the play centers naturally on the king and queen, but the other characters, from Madrassy down to Jakab, are all extremely well portrayed. Madrassy is wily and subtle. Once the king's tutor in classics, he was later made minister of education. During the Red Terror of the revolution he was conveniently ill with rheumatic fever, and during the succeeding White Terror he had shingles; so by avoiding politics he has remained in office. He agrees when the queen calls him an opportunist. He is a politician, not a soldier, and somewhat of a scholar, too. He has arranged for some school children with rickets to be examined and thus has helped a scientist learn about the disease. Timer-server that he is, he is not happy. Yet something in him causes him to seek power, though once in power he is a helpless prisoner of those who put him there, as the king points out.

Bruckner is another type of opportunist. He says little during the first part of the play, letting Madrassy do the talking. Unlike Madrassy, he is for fighting and deciding once and for all who is master of the country. He admits that he means to be master himself. He has no scruples. He suggests that the king's party take advantage of the armistice to surprise the enemy. When the queen tries to bribe him with her pearls, he confesses that he can be bought, but she does not have the price at this time. After he has Czernyak killed, he comes to the king to suggest an alliance. The king, when Bruckner bends over to undo a package, recognizes him suddenly by the top of his head as a former bootblack who always read a great deal and who was given help to go to the university. During the war he has been imprisoned—for optimism, he says, for believing that men are brothers and can make a better world. He says he is quite over this naiveté now, and his lack of scruples and desire for power show clearly that he is no longer an idealist. He could use the king because the king is an impressive figure, and more than that, because there is a mutual liking between him and the people, which Bruckner cannot say of himself. He cynically suggests that the people must be kept busy working and fighting, but their ideas must not be allowed to become dangerous.

Among the king's supporters, Count Czernyak is outstanding in his hot-headed, impulsive desire to fight to reinstate the king. He is a Carpathian Hotspur. His mother, the Countess Czernyak, is the former governess of the queen and is completely loyal to her, though she wishes the king had not returned to the country. Her own country home, where their majesties find shelter on their return, has been looted and wrecked by the populace in the madness of the revolution, and she says her life is in ruins, too. It is she who expresses what might be called the basic idea of the play when she says: "They should never have come back. It was hopeless. That world has vanished." After her son's death she is content to go with the queen into exile because the queen is the only one left whom she loves except her daughter Dominica. Dominica elects to stay in Carpathia, though the queen tries to persuade her to leave, because it is her country.

One of the best-drawn minor characters is old Colonel Hadik. Once an expert artillery man, he now anxiously asks for a less responsible appointment because he is not sure that one should kill. So he becomes a servant to the king and queen during their brief return to their country.

The mayor of the town of Zimony, where the king is staying,

expresses the attitude of the ordinary citizen toward the return of their majesties. He is on the side of the king personally, but what good is to come of all the fighting? He had thought that the king's return would bring peace to the land, but it has not. All the ordinary person wants, he says, is to be left alone with what good remains to him.

With these and other characters Barker presents vividly the disturbed condition of the land after the war and the various attitudes of its people. These individuals and attitudes are found not only in the mythical Carpathia, but they are probably fairly universal after any war. One anonymous English reviewer comments on the fact that there is an English flavor to this play because of its "tolerant wit" and "urbane" statesmen.[11] Though the play may seem especially English in character, England surely has no monopoly on tolerance and wit in her statesmen. It is to Barker's credit at any rate that mythical kingdom though Carpathia is, its citizens and their problems are made to seem very real.

Like the rest of Barker's work, this play is carefully detailed. There is much accurate observation of society and of human nature in it and much thought, and an excellent expression of this observation and thought. In dialogue and curtains it is naturalistic. The speech suggests real life in its style, for the speakers are not always clear and logical. The exposition is smoothly presented, and, unlike some other of Barker's works, this play is easy to understand from the very first. The exiled king is being interviewed by an American correspondent at the beginning, and thus we learn the situation. There is a beautiful rounding out of the whole when at the end the king reads the interview as he is riding in the train which is taking him into permanent exile, the interview in which he stated that he had no intention of going back to Carpathia. The settings are effective: the ruined chateau of act 2, lit by candles; the railway station headquarters of the king in act 3; the railway carriage of act 4, which jerks and bumps as the train starts up. There are scenes of dramatic intensity: the decision of the king to return, just after his wife resignedly suggests that he abdicate; his throwing down of his sword in surrender when his troops disobey orders; the news of Czernyak's death. There is more appeal to the emotions and less academic discussion than in *The Voysey Inheritance, Waste,* or *The Madras House.* The scene between the queen and Jakab, for example, and the queen's distress at having to leave as a failure (as she believes) are poignant and convincing. And above all, the wonderfully live characters show the hand of the skilled dramatist. In the stage directions Barker continues his practice of addressing the reader and giving valuable details which could not be directly depicted on the stage but which would contribute to a finished actor's performance.

Realistic though the play is in its approach to its subject, yet there are elements in it suggesting the romantic side of Barker which was present as early as *The Marrying of Ann Leete* and which revealed itself in the two collaborations, *Prunella* and *The Harlequinade*, and in *Farewell to the Theatre*. The setting in a mythical kingdom and the concern with royalty place *His Majesty* apart from Barker's earlier realistic presentations of English middle-class life. The very fact that European royalty with any power is a thing of the past and that Barker treats his royalty sympathetically gives almost a nostalgic atmosphere to the work. There is some symbolism here, but it is less detailed than in *The Secret Life*, and what there is is directly pointed out to us. Countess Czernyak, for example, tells us that her life is like the wreckage of her home, and Madrassy comments on the symbolic effect of their majesties living in a train without an engine. The king might appear to be something of a romantic figure in the idealism which causes him to abdicate his throne regardless of his wife's feelings and his own material loss. But Barker's fidelity to the truth leads him to show us that the king is not really unhappy about giving up a job which is difficult in the dangerously unsettled times, especially since he has been able to accomplish his aim of preventing civil war.

That *His Majesty* has not been produced cannot be due to any obscurity or difficulty in the play itself, as might with justice be said of *The Secret Life*. It has excellent character portrayal, unity of theme and plot, much dramatic conflict, theatrically effective settings, an interesting subject, and good dialogue. One can agree with the anonymous reviewer who said: " 'His Majesty' is an important play and should be produced by our most important producer, its author."[12] Unfortunately Barker never staged the play nor to this date has anyone else.

Are these last two of Barker's plays in any sense autobiographical?

Although, as with *Farewell to the Theatre*, one can easily go too far with this sort of speculation, it is tempting to agree, partly, at least, with C. B. Purdom that they are. There are similarities between Evan Strowde's withdrawal from active political life and his reluctance to return to it and Barker's retirement from the theater. Like Strowde, who found out that his vision of the world was not like the reality, Barker perhaps had to admit that his vision of what the theater could be like was not going to be realized, at least in the immediate future. As for *His Majesty*, Purdom suggests that King Henry of Carpathia is "a final self-dramatization."[13] There undoubtedly can be seen in Barker's description of the king some of Barker's own traits: *"He is not a very handsome man, nor probably a very clever man; but he is shrewd. His courtesy is innate and he has an ironic, a mischievous sense of humor. He has charm. There are depths in him too; for at times, one may notice, he withdraws into himself, seems to withdraw altogether elsewhere."* After having done his best to achieve his purpose, the king returns to private life with his wife and his chickens. Barker, too, after a very active life in the world of the theater, withdrew from it almost entirely to live with his wife and his writing.

Chapter Seven

Dramatist, Mainly Realistic

In the early twentieth century Granville Barker was an important figure among the "new" dramatists, between whose work and the conventional well-made play there were marked differences. According to Barker the popular plays had forced out of the English theater audience everybody over the mental age of twenty-five, and this audience could be recaptured only by more intelligent plays.[1] Shaw had earlier insisted that there was "no future now for any drama without music except the drama of thought" because music can so much better appeal to the emotions. He maintained that the popular drama of the day, in trying to affect the emotions like opera, had become vapidly sentimental, that its characters behaved not realistically but according "to the romantic logic of the stage."[2] (Although at this time neither Shaw nor Barker could speak of the motion picture as a medium of entertainment, they might have added not much later than this that the theater also cannot hope to compete with films in dramas of physical action or spectacle.) Thus in their view only one type of play remained for the stage: that which appealed to the intellect with an intelligent presentation of problems and ideas and the careful portrayal of character. In the presentation of this type of work the theater has an undisputed place in our lives.

It is in this realm of the intellectual play that Barker made his notable contributions. Whether he is writing of the eighteenth-century Ann Leete or the twentieth-century King Henry XIII of Carpathia, he is dealing intellectually with some facet of our civilization. His plays are of interest and value for what his characters say more than for what they do, although he does characterize through action as well as talk. He gives us a detailed view of English middle-class life, presenting it in a predominantly unfavorable light. His plays offer a more complete picture of English politics than any other modern dramatist has presented; they suggest that the idealist in politics runs into much opposition. He deals with various aspects of the question of the status of women in society and shows the powerful effect of the Life Force on human relationships. He is critical of conventional education, which teaches false values.

These are the prominent themes in Barker's plays. He reveals himself as an idealist, always sincere, thoughtful, and intelligent, doing battle with hypocrisy, false morality, selfish politics, blind education, middle-class smugness. His heroes are all of a pattern, and that pattern is much like Barker himself. To Barker, life is not simple; the separation between right and wrong is not clearly marked. There is always uncertainty; there are complications; there is no easy answer to the question of what is good and what is bad. Society is complex, and his intellectual characters are aware of its complexity. They are analytical in their attitude. They examine the world and find it wanting; they examine their own emotions, motives, and actions. With their idealism there is a detached coolness about them which makes them more admirable intellectually than affecting emotionally. They have a clarity of perception and are good commentators on the people and ideas surrounding them. They want to improve society and have ideas of their own which they propound earnestly and intelligently, but they must first think and talk rather than acting on the spur of the moment.

Ashley Dukes aptly calls the leading character in Barker's plays the "hero-raisonneur," and suggests that after Shaw destroyed the hero of the old plays, Barker tried putting him together again "upon strictly Shavian lines, dispassionately and without romance." He suffers, however, from too much intelligence, says Dukes; he is bent on discovering a point of view, an attitude. This sets him apart from Shaw's characters, who are quite certain of themselves.[3]

Yet though they talk a lot, Barker's heroes are not completely paralyzed when it comes to action. Edward Voysey assumes his unpleasant burden, Trebell commits suicide, Philip Madras makes a break from the women's clothing business to run for the County Council, Evan Strowde returns to politics at least temporarily, and King Henry quells the civil war in his kingdom before abdicating. These heroes, thinkers though they are, are no mere idle thinkers. They all have at least intellectual passion, and it is that which drives them to try to make their world better.

Dickinson finds that despite Barker's positive qualities of intelligence and technical skill, "he has one lack, this being the sense of conviction, or of the worth-while, which would have made him one of the greatest dramatists of our time."[4] It is true, notably in *The Madras House*, that the weakest part of the plays dramatically is the hero's exposition of his constructive ideas about society. It is true also that Barker presents many different points of view, many different aspects of the problems facing his characters in their complex world. Because of this method of contrasting ideas it may seem that he himself lacks a sense of conviction about what is worthwhile. Actually this is not so.

Barker's personal philosophy is inevitably revealed in a careful study of several of his plays. Though he emphasizes the complexities of life, the difficulty of knowing exactly what is right, the underlying theme of his plays is one of idealism and hope. His heroes are all sincerely striving for the good, however hidden and tortuous the road to it may be. With Trebell, Barker believes in the power of education and in eventual progress, though the precise goal itself may not be clear. With Philip Madras, he may hate "that farmyard world of sex" and dislike giving up beauty and entrusting one's life to the still undeveloped minds of the masses in democracy, but with Philip he knows that this one must do if civilization is to advance. The better equipped and better educated must take an active part in politics and in bringing culture to the whole of society. One cannot try to stop the forward movement of time and go back to a vanished age as Queen Rosamund would like to do. Democracy is the civilized world of the future, and for the full achievement of its possibilities for human happiness and culture, one must accept one's responsibilities. One cannot retire to the sidelines as Evan Strowde attempts to do; one cannot refuse to do nature's work like the selfish, cowardly Amy O'Connell. As is evident from *The Marrying of Ann Leete* and *Prunella*, one cannot fight nature; our natural emotions are right while the artificial conventions of society have faults. These are Barker's convictions as they appear in his plays, though he does not, in his presentation of life as an artist, write only or even mainly for the purpose of using the stage as a pulpit.

Some of Barker's heroines are quite as conscious of the world as his heroes, and quite as dispassionate and intellectual. Alice Maitland, Barker's best example of the New Woman, is not a very attractive person because of her coldness. Beatrice Voysey expresses ideas suggestive of the New Woman, but she is one who has been embittered and hardened by poverty. Jessica Madras is the aestheticized creature of good manners, good taste,and blindness to the ugliness and unhappiness of the world that Philip does not want his daughter to become.

But there are other women in Barker, too, different in various ways from these and sometimes warmer and more attractive. Ann Leete is one who does not explain her actions and beliefs at length; she simply acts most directly. Amy O'Connell has no great virtues as a woman: she is not intellectual nor is she brave; she would rather kill herself than bear her child. Miss Yates is not an intellectual woman either, but she is proud of performing her function in the world by having a child. Dorothy Taverner is admirable in her sacrifice of financial and popular success for artistic integrity. Joan Westbury, in her refusal of Evan without knowing why exactly but because something in her inner secret self prompts her to, has more of the mystic quality which Ann Leete suggests. Eleanor Strowde and Frances Trebell are both faithful sisters to heroes, though Eleanor is the more intellectual and idealistic of the two. Queen Rosamund is thoroughly human in her foolishness, her pride, and withal her warm heart and courage. One might say in summing up Barker's leading women characters that the New Woman he does not succeed in making attractive, but the old-fashioned women are believable and charming, despite (or perhaps because of) the weaknesses they have.

Characters other than his heroes and heroines Barker portrays with consummate skill. The elder Voysey, for example, is fascinating; and though Mrs. Voysey, who has lived quietly for some time with the knowledge of her husband's dishonesty, is less important, she is completely believable. Edward's brothers are carefully differentiated and all true to life. The gallery of memorable personages is long—Mr. Huxtable with his wife and his ménage of daughters; Constantine Madras and his conventional but wronged wife; Oliver Gauntlett, bitter and disillusioned; the hot-blooded Czernyak and the faithful countess, his mother; old Jakab. All of these come to mind immediately as realistically defined individuals.

Barker's interest in his characters is analytic, but he always shows sympathy for them. The reprehensible persons are made understandable through his insight; the idealistic ones are generally not obnoxiously self-righteous or self-confident. Even in the portrayal of the mentally impoverished Huxtables there is pity mingled with satire. The character for whom Barker seems to feel least sympathy is Amy O'Connell, but because of Trebell's coldness toward her we can pity even her.

It is not only in the depiction of individuals that Barker excels; his studies of groups of people are perhaps even more striking. Several families are found in the various plays, and the outstanding scenes are those in which entire groups take part. The family gathering after the wedding of Ann and Abud is only the first of such group portraits. The Voyseys gathered to hear Edward's startling revelation about their father, the politicians debating Trebell's moral standing and his usefulness to them, the Huxtables at home together, the discussion about women at the Madras House, the politicians at the seaside home of Evan Strowde—all of these are outstanding scenes not only in Barker's plays but among the plays of the time. The interplay of ideas and personalities in them makes them amusing, provocative, and theatrically effective. Barker belongs to the problem-play school of dramatists in a sense, but more than presenting a specific problem he creates a detailed picture of a social milieu, with a prevailing mood of decadence[5] or disillusion.

Artificial, though admittedly useful to a degree, are such labels as "realist," "naturalist," and "romanticist." In any precise sense Barker is difficult to classify. He is generally realistic in his choice of subject and in his attitude toward life; he is predominantly naturalistic in technique; but there are suggestions of the romanticist in him, too.

Compared to those of the continental naturalists, Barker's plays are more intellectual in style and content and more idealistic in tone. Their effect is not depressing but intellectually stimulating. Yet his method as a dramatist is mainly naturalistic. There is nothing theatrical in his dialogue or his curtains. There are no operatic aria speeches as in Shaw, though the characters speak with a more intellectual quality than do Galsworthy's, for in general they are more refined and intelligent. The exposition is so naturalistic at times (in *The Marrying of Ann Leete*, *Waste*, and *The Secret Life*, for example) that at the beginning of the play one does not know exactly what is going on. But in other plays, though still not using obviously artificial devices, Barker gives us a very clear idea of what we need to know. In *The Voysey Inheritance*, for example, the elder Voysey at the beginning explains his true financial situation to his son. In act 1 of *His Majesty* there is the completely acceptable device of a reporter interviewing the exiled king. Through these bits of dialogue the necessary information is given to the audience.

Information during the course of the play is given in a subtle way, too. P. P. Howe cites a good example of Barker's unobtrusive technique. He says that even "Ibsen himself may be caught hammer in hand driving home a point" that we must not miss, but Barker never does. In *Waste*, for instance, we learn about the fate of a leading character through a subordinate clause in a question: "But since Mrs. O'Connell is dead what is the excuse for a scandal?" Howe concludes: "For the technical improvement, at least, in the contemporary English drama, the credit is more Mr. Granville Barker's than any man's."[6] In *The Voysey Inheritance* we learn that the elder Voysey has died between acts 2 and 3 by the dress of the characters, the special luncheon on the dining room table and the neatness of the room, the solicitude of old Booth for the family, and remarks which only indirectly inform us about what has taken place. Barker's dialogue (except in *Prunella* and *The Harlequinade*, which are fantasies) is naturalistic in the flow of question and answer (or no answer), unfinished sentences, shifts of subject, or continuation of a speech by a character though others have interposed unrelated remarks. Each character talks as we would expect a person of his position and background to talk. There are no soliloquies or asides.

With respect to "curtains" Barker is naturalistic, too. There is not a single melodramatic or contrived concluding speech in the plays. The closest he comes to such a speech is Walter's comment at the end of *Waste* expressing his anger at the tragic loss of a good man, and even this is appropriate. Furthest in the direction of naturalism is the ending of *The Madras House*, where the fall of the curtain concludes the conversation between Philip and Jessica, not because they have reached a conclusion, for actually the discussion has no end, but because the play must end somewhere. There is always (except in *Waste*) the feeling of life going on after the play ends; the ending never consists of the final rewarding of virtue and punishing of villainy and the clearing up of all loose ends. Indeed there is not even a villain. Not all characters are equally idealistic, but all, from Carnaby Leete to Madrassy in *His Majesty*, are understandable and recognizable human beings.

Despite his attention to realistic detail, Barker, like any true artist, is not a mere photographer or recorder of real life. Every bit of detail serves a purpose either in the characterization of an individual, in the presentation of a group, or in the creation of atmosphere, although not all critics have recognized this fact. Some have complained that there is so much detail in Barker's plays and so much talk that the real significance is lost sight of.[7] It is undeniable that there is much detail and much talk in Barker's plays, that he refuses to conform to the conventions of the well-made play, that he does not attempt to make things crystal clear at once, that his plays are not a substitute for a good cigar or a game at dominoes to an idle man. But it is equally apparent to the careful and sympathetic reader that they are not at all haphazardly thrown together, that every detail contributes something, though its purpose may not be immediately seen, that Barker has much to say about life that is worth hearing, that he interprets and does not merely reproduce life.

Realism in subject matter and naturalism in method are characteristic especially of the plays of what might be termed Barker's middle period (that is, *The Voysey Inheritance*, *Waste*, and *The Madras House*); but there is an element of the romantic and of the imaginative, too, which is found as early as *The Marrying of Ann Leete*. The atmosphere of the garden just before dawn when reality is for the time hidden in blackness is in keeping with the strangeness of the hidden force in Ann which causes her to rebel against the dictates of her practical father and suddenly propose to the young gardener. The suggestions of symbolism in the touches of darkness and light, the voices of the future children of Ann and Abud heard only by her at the end, the beauty of the final scene of Ann being lighted up the stairs by her new husband—these are hints of Barker's imaginative powers. *Prunella* is admittedly a fantasy and makes full use of symbolism, allegory, and unreal devices such as the statue of Love coming to life. In *The Voysey Inheritance*, *Waste*, and *The Madras House* the realist conquers the romanticist almost entirely, but not quite. There are the elder Voysey's roses, for example. In *Waste* Trebell's sudden awareness of his need for his child is another hint of the secret inner life which has motivated Ann Leete's behavior and which later achieves its full importance in Joan Westbury. The fabulous Constantine Madras is really a romantic character.

The Harlequinade is not at all realistic in method or subject matter, and especially in the fifteenth-century pantomime episode it gives full scope to the romantic appeal of the theater in creating a world of magic quite different from the plain, everyday middle-class existence of the Voyseys and the Huxtables. Dorothy Taverner's mystic conversations with her voices at Braxted Abbey are another indication of the imaginative element in Barker. In *The Secret Life* this imaginative element supersedes the realistic. Realism there is in dialogue and characterization, but there is something more spiritual here than in the earlier plays. The dramatist's interest has definitely broadened from a detailed study of problems of society and of politics, though politics is ostensibly the subject matter of the play, to the more significant topic of the human soul in the vastness of the universe. Though the stage represents a loggia, a gallery, a room, yet the dramatist looks far beyond these restrictions to the world of the artist. There are touches of symbolism as in *The Marrying of Ann Leete*; there is a development of the idea of the inner life which prompts one's actions, but which cannot be explained even to oneself, to say nothing of others. In the dialogue there is a great deal of poetic beauty which gives the work a lyrical quality far removed from the realism of *The Voysey Inheritance* and *The Madras House*. In *His Majesty* Barker continues to show his romantic side in the setting in mythical Carpathia and in the royal hero and heroine, though the dialogue and the subject matter are not so imaginative as in *The Secret Life*.

This shift in emphasis away from realism to the more imaginative is a shift seen around 1920 in the work of other dramatists of the period, too, but it is in a way a broadening of Barker's own outlook, or a freeing of an aspect of his art which is evident from the beginning. Barker's work as a producer, especially of Shakespeare, shows his imaginative power as well. John Palmer, who hailed *The Marrying of Ann Leete* as being as rich in promise as a first play as *Love's Labour's Lost* but who was disappointed in Barker's next three plays, must have been pleased to see Barker breaking away to some extent in his last plays from the influence of realism, for he believed that the fact that Barker "in his impressionable years fell into the hands of Mr. Shaw and Mr. Galsworthy is a tragedy of English dramatic literature."[8] Whether one considers it unfortunate or not that Barker chose to write realistic plays depends, of course, upon one's own taste. One must, however, recognize that he did fine work in a variety of types. Truth to tell, he was an experimentalist in the drama.

Any discussion of Barker's plays must contain a special word about his stage directions and the literary quality of his work. Following the example of Shaw, who believed that both the actor and the reader of the published play need to know more about the personal and social background of the characters than was customarily given in order to understand the dialogue and the action, Barker from his first play to his last provided complete and detailed stage directions.

George P. Baker was of the opinion that Barker's type of full stage directions are needless because the information in them will come out in the text; or, if it does not, then the text of the play is faulty.[9] William Archer also believed that the author should not intrude in the stage directions.[10] Theoretically and ideally these criticisms of expanded stage directions may be true, but Barker's interpolated remarks are generally so skillful and so in tune with the play that they are not intrusions at all. They are not polemic as Shaw's are at times, nor are they embarrassingly whimsical as Barrie's may be. They include information which cannot be directly conveyed on the stage, but they are consistent with Barker's belief as a producer that the actors should know the characters they are portraying completely and in detail, not simply be able to memorize and recite their lines; and they certainly help the reader create in his imagination the warmth, color, movement, inflection of voice, power of gesture, and through them the total emotional and intellectual effect, which the stage performance would supply. Besides, Barker's stage directions are always written in a graceful literary style which, added to the effective presentation of ideas important to civilized society through the words and actions of a variety of convincingly drawn characters, helps to give his plays lasting value as literature.

The practice of writing expanded stage directions and the high literary quality of the plays of Shaw, Barrie, and Barker are significantly related to the passing in 1891 of the American Copyright Bill, which insured similar protection to printed works in America as in England. Dickinson points out that the result of this action was the printing of more plays, and he states: "The two foundation stones upon which rest the drama of the early twentieth century are the experimental theatre and the printed play."[11] That plays could be published with copyright protection after 1891 accounts, in part at any rate, for the higher literary quality of the dialogue and for the expanded stage directions in the works of these dramatists. Conversely, because the plays of Shaw, Barrie, and Barker have literary merit, they can survive as printed works apart from stage presentation.

The influence of Shaw on Barker as a dramatist is evident, then, in his use of expanded stage direction, and also in the intellectual quality of his plays. There are suggestions of Shaw in the New Women of Barker, in the background ideas of Socialism (Philip Madras, for example, insists that we must base our culture on the well-being of all), in the criticisms of middle-class education, morality, and culture, in the lack of action and abundance of talk.

The differences between the two dramatists, however, are equally apparent. First, Barker lacks the brilliant wit of Shaw. Touches of humor there are in Barker, but it is a quiet humor with nothing of the pyrotechnic quality of Shaw. Second, Barker gives more of an impression of thoughtful sincerity and moderation than Shaw. Shaw's attitude seems so flippant that one wonders at times if he can be serious. Third, Barker never gives the impression of being unfailingly sure of himself. He analyzes problems from many different points of view, balancing them one against the other and seeing good points in many of them. With Shaw there is no hesitance; he is right and he knows it. Fourth, Barker's characters are convincingly realistic individuals, and their dialogue is natural and true to character. Shaw seems not so much concerned with realism of character and dialogue as with expressing himself, and any or all of his characters may serve as his mouthpieces in long operatic aria speeches.

Shaw himself did not consider Barker to be an imitator of him. In answer to the question: "Do you think Barker was an imitator of Shaw?" he wrote: "No. We could not have been less alike. He had never seen great acting, and hated it, whereas I, having seen it in my boyhood and been stagestruck by it, always wrote for it. He used to say to the company when I was rehearsing 'Remember, will you, that this is Italian Opera.' His own style was lowtoned; and even in his Shakespear [*sic*] productions the big parts were underplayed. Galsworthy was the author for him."[12]

There is a certain similarity between Barker and Galsworthy in their detachment, their presentation of several sides of a problem, and their very concern with problems. But here again appear significant differences. Barker's dialogue is more intellectual in content and style because there are more intellectuals among his characters. As in dialogue, so in the entire construction of the play Barker is much more complex than Galsworthy, more subtle and more delicate. Galsworthy's plays are clear-cut, direct, logical, easy to understand. Barker's have suggestions of things left unsaid, they probe deeper into their characters, their plan is less obvious, and therefore they are sometimes difficult to read.

Other possible influences on Barker may be noted. The realism of Ibsen and his emphasis on the emancipation of woman certainly paved the way for Barker and his contemporaries, as did the naturalism of Hauptmann. Among English dramatists, Robertson, Pinero, and Jones, old-fashioned though they may seem beside Barker, did take steps toward the presentations of the problems of real life on the stage. There is a Meredithian flavor to the intellectual comedy of Barker in its occasional obscurity and in its dependence for humor not on farcical situations or horseplay but on the ironies of life and the characters' unawareness of their true selves. Harold Williams suggests that though Barker "was probably in no way a conscious disciple of [James], . . . his prolix, involved and somewhat chilling intellectual drama is in the same class in workmanship as Henry James's novels."[13] There is definitely a suggestion of Chekhov in Barker's technique of creating atmosphere through the use of detail, in the fact that the drama in his plays is internal rather than external, and in the careful though seemingly haphazard construction. That Barker admired Chekhov is apparent in his critical writings. One can see some of Maeterlinck's use of symbolism in Barker, too, and some of his romantic atmosphere, especially in his last plays.

At best, however, the determining of influences on a writer's work is uncertain, though similarities can be pointed out in tone, style, subject matter, and so on. Similarities exist between Barker's work as a dramatist and that of others, but he is not an imitator of anyone. He has great insight, intellectual ability, and originality. His plays are distinctively Granville Barker's.

Original as they are in insight and skillful in execution, why have Barker's plays not proved more popular? One reason undoubtedly is that they possess an intellectual quality rather than a quickly felt emotional appeal, a subtlety in dialogue at times which William Archer found incomprehensible in the earliest of them. Their interest lies in characterization and ideas rather than in the obvious theatricalities of the well-made play. The talk is about philosophy, morality, politics; and it does not have Shaw's wit to relieve its seriousness. The plays demand an alert audience or reader; they cannot be skimmed through rapidly. Merely the great number of characters in each of the major works requires concentration from the reader just to keep the individuals straight in one's mind—a difficulty which would certainly be eased in a performance with the actual individuals seen and heard on the stage. This need for a large cast is, of course, a drawback from the point of view of commercial production. Barker's are ideally plays for a national repertory company subsidized by the government.

Barker's total output of published original dramatic work is not very large—six full-length plays, three one-act plays, and two collaborations. It must be remembered, however, that up to the time of World War I he was actively engaged in acting and producing as well as writing; so the wonder is not that he did relatively little writing in those years but that he found time to do so much. After he retired from his active work in the theater, nevertheless, it seems that he might have written more original plays had he wanted to. Earlier he had expressed the desire to have more time for writing, but when the time came after the war, he wrote only two one-act plays (*Vote by Ballot* and *Farewell to the Theatre*) and two full-length plays (*The Secret Life* and *His Majesty*). Not that he was idle by any means, for he translated a number of plays with his second wife, he worked for a national theater in England, and he contributed much valuable Shakespearian criticism; but of original playwriting there is relatively little in the last thirty years of his life, with no new plays published after 1929.

One reason for the small quantity of Barker's original dramatic work is undoubtedly the fact that writing was not easy for him. Shaw says of Barker: "He wrote slowly and with difficulty. . . . When his *Madras House* was in rehearsal he hung it up for weeks because he could not write the scene between Constantine and his wife. At last I wrote it myself; and this so infuriated him (as I knew it would) that he finished it in a day in his own manner."[14]

After Barker's divorce from Lillah McCarthy and his marriage to Helen Manchester Huntington, he no longer had Shaw to prod him into writing, for the second Mrs. Barker did not approve of the Socialist Shaw, and Barker almost never saw him again. Shaw's feelings toward the second Mrs. Barker were bitter. "His marriage to Mrs. Huntingdon [*sic*] was his divorce from me," he says. "It finished him politically and artistically. She had a very considerable literary talent; but it stopped at Meredith and Henry James; and to her all Socialists were infamous guttersnipes. She hated me, and was determined to rescue him from my evil and disgraceful influence." Shaw adds somewhat uncharitably, "And her alimony from Huntingdon was more than sufficient for Barker to live on opulently."[15] Not only did the second Mrs. Barker not approve of Shaw, but, according to Shaw, neither did she approve of Barker's early plays. "I hope," observes Shaw, "his widow has come to see that the wild oats he sowed with me have produced a better harvest than she foresaw, and that his original contributions to our dramatic literature are treasures to be preserved, not compromising documents to be destroyed."[16] What Mrs. Barker wanted apparently had a great influence on Barker—at least if we are to believe Shaw, who says, "What surprised me was that he was completely and abjectly under her thumb; for at the Court he liked to have his own way."[17] Exactly how Shaw knew this about Barker's relationship with his wife he does not reveal, for his own intimacy with Barker had ended.

Here are two explanations, then, for the relatively small quantity of Barker's original dramatic output—his slowness in writing and the influence of the second Mrs. Barker. The first seems reasonable; the second, based as it is on Shaw's emotionally colored statement, is perhaps less to be relied upon.

A third possible reason can be found in the mood of disillusion after the war which Barker portrays so skillfully in Evan Strowde in *The Secret Life* and which may be a reflection of his own mood. His earlier plays had received at best a mixed reception, some critics arguing academically that *The Madras House*, for example, was not a play at all, because it was unconventional in its structure. His last three plays were not produced, Barker himself having retired from that phase of theatrical activity and no one else apparently being interested enough in the theater apart from its commercial aspects to stage them. His ardent attempts to establish a national theater had come to naught. It is understandable that Barker, always a perfectionist, not having received more encouragement, might have decided that to continue what was at best difficult was not worth the effort. In *The Use of the Drama*, published in the year before his death, Barker complained about the fact that there was no real theater in England or in America. He spoke about a man he knew who had in his most active years been busy in various aspects of theatrical work but who had not been seen or heard from for some time. "I asked him when I met him some time later, 'Why did you leave the theater?' He answered me, 'Because there was none to leave.' "[18] This man he knew sounds very much like Barker himself.

Certainly Barker the dramatist had not written himself out. *The Secret Life* and *His Majesty*, rather than suggesting that their author is merely rehashing earlier ideas, go on to new depths of understanding and thought. On the other hand, Barker in his later work, at least in the Shakespeare criticism, was writing about a subject that had always been of great interest to him. So it was not exactly a situation in which Barker with a feeling of hopelessness dropped one kind of activity to go on to something different, but rather a development of another aspect of his varied work related to the theater and the drama. Dixon Scott expresses the view that the real Barker is not the actor and producer but the writer: "He is just as much an actor-manager as Shakespeare was; not more. His natural kingdom is between boards, not upon them."[19] This emphasis on Barker the dramatist is a welcome one; yet his plays are only a part, albeit a very significant one, of his work in the theater. The various aspects of his career—acting, producing, writing plays and criticism—were interrelated and influential one upon the other, and are all evidence of a total interest in the theater.

As an original dramatist, what are Barker's contributions and what is his importance? One cannot say that he established a school of followers, but one can claim that in his earlier works he contributed to the advancement of realism-naturalism in the English drama and carried that technique even further than his contemporaries. He helped to free the English drama from the constraints of the well-made play, to bring it into closer contact with the realities of life. He experimented with dramatic forms and helped to expand the idea of what could be considered a play. He helped to broaden the scope of the drama by introducing subject matter previously considered morally unsuitable, as in *Waste*, and subject matter from everyday life, as in *The Madras House*. In his last plays (unproduced though they were), particularly in *The Secret Life*, he showed the way to a more spiritual and symbolic drama, still within the naturalistic technique.

He helped to raise the level of dramatic writing by creating plays that have intellectual and literary value as well as theatrical effect, plays which are still interesting for their ideas. He contributed detailed and significant studies, with many memorable scenes, of English middle-class life and of English politics. In this he is without a peer. He created many fascinating characters and emphasized the psychological study of character probably to a greater extent than any of his contemporaries. He wrote plays which are important in themselves as fine dramatic works. And finally, he helped raise the dramatist to a position of greater importance than the actors who impersonated the people of the play. As St. John Ervine says, the English dramatists of the early twentieth century, Barker among them, "rushed through the stage door of the English theatre and made the actors take the count. . . . the dramatic critics, led by William Archer, ceased to be interested in acting and wrote only of the play."[20]

Had Barker written more than a half-dozen original plays, he would undoubtedly have achieved a reputation as a major English dramatist. The plays that he did write, however, are sufficient to insure him a permanent position as a dramatist of great originality, powerful intellect, extraordinary understanding of human nature, and skill of technique and literary expression far above the average. Barker's dream of a national theater for England was fulfilled by its establishment in 1963; its magnificent new building complex was opened in 1976. The successful production by the National Theatre thus far of two of Barker's plays, *The Marrying of Ann Leete* in 1975 and *The Madras House* in 1977, is a happy indication that his plays will continue to live and that his reputation as a dramatist may even be enhanced. If that is so, his high standing will be well deserved.

Chapter Eight
Critic, Idealistic and Practical

As well as contributing to the modern theater as actor, producer, and dramatist, Granville Barker wrote a considerable amount of criticism. After his retirement from active work in the theater itself, he wrote books, articles, and prefaces; and he delivered lectures, later published, in which he expressed his ideas about the drama in general, about acting and playwriting, and about individual writers, chiefly Shakespeare. The most important of these works are *Scheme and Estimates for a National Theatre* (written in collaboration with William Archer, first published privately in 1904), *The Exemplary Theatre* (1922), *A National Theatre* (a complete rewriting of the *Scheme and Estimates* by Barker alone, 1930), *On Dramatic Method* (1931), *The Study of Drama* (1934), *On Poetry in Drama* (1937), *The Use of the Drama* (1945), and *Prefaces to Shakespeare* (several in different editions beginning with prefaces to acting editions of *The Winter's Tale* and *Twelfth Night* in 1912, and *A Midsummer Night's Dream* in 1914). Barker believed that criticism has an important function in the advancement of all the arts, but especially theatrical art.[1] His comments are of special value because they are the comments of a man with practical experience in the theater, not simply those of a playgoer, a reader of plays, or a theorist.

The theme of the value of drama in the development of a civilized society and specifically in education continually recurs in Barker's writings. It is not surprising that Barker, who often has the characters in his plays criticize society and education, should reveal these concerns when he speaks in his own person. Because of the drama's interest in fundamental truth and in human beings in their relations with one another in society, Barker firmly believes that drama has an immense educational value. This idea forms a major portion of his book *The Exemplary Theatre* and is the subject of two shorter works, *The Study of Drama* and *The Use of the Drama*.

In *The Exemplary Theatre*, the earliest of these works, Barker points out, as he does elsewhere, that one of the important aspects of the drama is that it requires cooperation. There must be cooperation between the dramatist and the actor, and the audience must contribute, too. There must be cooperation among the actors themselves. Each character must be fully developed, but what each actor must be primarily concerned with is the entire play, not his own individual opportunity to shine. This idea is, of course, a statement of Barker's own philosophy and practice as a producer. Being thus a cooperative effort, the drama can contribute greatly to the civilization of man by increasing his understanding of society, which is also a cooperative undertaking.[2] But the drama interprets life as well as reflecting it. "It is its shadow," says Barker, "but then it is its illumination, too." For we gain vicarious experience through participating in the play as spectators, and we acquire an understanding of human nature. "It is not out of ourselves the dramatist must needs take us, but rather a little further in."[3] Moreover, we have a community of interest and a sympathy not only with the characters in the play but also with our neighbors in the theater. One indication that a performance is successful, Barker suggests, is seen when strangers at the play talk to one another about it during an intermission.[4]

In *The Exemplary Theatre* Barker also discusses topics such as the art of acting and of producing, the characteristics of various playwrights, and conditions in the contemporary theater. A major portion of the work is devoted, however, as the title would indicate, to describing an ideal theater, which consists partly of a school for the study of drama and partly of a kind of national theater, a playhouse for the performance of works in repertory.

Barker visualizes a theater school which would have two kinds of students—those who are aiming to become professionals in the theater (a relatively small number) and those who are studying drama for its general educational value, who may perhaps become administrators of community theaters or teachers of drama in the schools—not teachers for the narrow purpose of developing actors, producers, or dramatists, but for the larger purpose of developing good citizens. In this school of the drama the actual performance of plays by students would be a minor part of the curriculum.[5] Instead the emphasis would be on the cooperative critical study of plays in seminars. The study of a play would follow a pattern like this: First the play would be read through aloud two or three times, with different readers for the different parts, in order to try to understand it. Then would follow a general discussion. Next specific persons would be chosen to interpret the parts; the addition of their personalities to the characters would bring about changes in interpretation. Then would come more discussion. The final step might occasionally be an actual production of the play, but the basic purpose of the seminar would be to work together to discover the play's meaning.[6]

Not all plays, in Barker's view, are equally suitable for this kind of study. There must be room for interpretation. *Candida, John Bull's Other Island, Strife,* and especially Chekhov's plays are very appropriate because there is so much left unsaid between the lines—in other words, they allow opportunity for discussion of differences of opinion.[7]

Later, in *The Use of the Drama*, where he recapitulates much of the material of the earlier work, Barker no longer links the study of plays with anything like a school of drama or a national theater, but rather speaks of it as part of a general educational program in the schools. He affirms his belief that a proper education in a democracy must not neglect the arts, including the drama. He does not advocate that the ordinary student try to become a practitioner in the arts and thus a "disappointed aesthete," rather that the arts be studied so as to develop the proper kind of citizen, one who will be "suitably articulate, keenly critical, fully appreciative." Barker does not believe in the arts only for entertainment; they have much wider powers. They can influence morals, though they should not be narrowly moralizing; they can liberate and at the same time discipline the imagination; they can provide a criterion of quality in all things.[8] The influence of the arts "gives a man poise, a point of view, sets up for him a general standard of quality. It helps refine his faculties, mature his precepts, gives balance to his judgment." The arts are not for only the selected few; they are of value to all citizens in preparing them to be able to select those few who will be their leaders.[9]

Although Barker believes in the educational benefits of studying a play without taking it to actual performance, yet he constantly reiterates that a play is not a play fully realized until it is presented on the stage by actors. To suggest that a play is more suitable for reading than for performance is a contradiction in terms. "As well praise a yacht for being built to stay safely in harbor as exalt a play because it is more fitted for the study than the stage."[10] One should read plays, of course, but always imagining them as they would appear on the stage.[11] The final bringing to life of a play is the performance of it, and thus in a very real sense, believes Barker, every play is a collaboration among dramatist, actor, and audience. Each has his own part to play in the cooperative effort.

The contribution of the actor is essential. Barker cites a performance of *The Cherry Orchard* at the Moscow Art Theater as an example of this fact. He felt that, having seen the performance, "to read the play afterwards was like reading the libretto of an opera—missing the music."[12] Since the dramatist has to work within certain limits of conciseness in presenting his characters and situation, he must suggest much by implication. For the full knowledge he needs for his part the actor must find out, through instinct or inference, what happened before the play began and what happens after the curtain falls. Moreover, it is not enough for just one actor to approach his part in this fashion; all must do it in cooperation.[13] Here Barker the critic reflects the practice of Barker the producer, who demanded just such an understanding of the character by the actor and whose productions at the Court Theatre and elsewhere were noted for their ensemble, not for individual star performances.

The producer has his function, too. He is like a conductor, says Barker, but he has less power than the conductor, since he is in control only at rehearsals.[14] From this cooperation with the playwright by actors and producer comes a creation of beauty which did not exist in any of the elements by itself.[15]

The final component of this tripartite cooperation upon which depends the full realization of the play is the audience, which is also essential. Without it, the best performance of the best play cannot be complete. The theater cannot advance so far that it leaves its audience behind.[16] The audience, for its part, must be willing to accept something more than "mere digestive entertainment"; it must learn to demand excellence in whatever kind of drama is being presented.[17]

It is apparent that the qualities which Barker demands of the playwright, actor, and audience are not those which are commonly found in the commercial theater, as he was well aware. These are ideals which the exemplary theater would strive for. In fact, there is no theater in England (or in America) which approaches the ideal, Barker complains in *The Exemplary Theatre*, for the playhouses are all controlled by commercial interests who are concerned only with appealing to the masses with anything that will sell.[18] Therefore he devotes approximately half of the book to describing a kind of national theater which would provide actors, producers, and everyone else necessary for the presentation of a play an opportunity to develop their craft and to perform great drama in repertory. To Barker a theater is not merely a building in which a play can be presented by a company formed for the purpose for as long as people will pay to see it. A building, and a well-equipped building, is certainly needed, but a theater above all involves "a stable organization of actors and actresses and directors, an institution in which the whole art of drama can be cultivated for its own sake and made manifest." A theater, he says, is like a library or a museum in its relation to the public and its services to the arts. The audience in such a theater would pay for its seats, and the numbers interested in attending any play would be important information to its directors, but the plays would not be chosen only for the purpose of attracting crowds any more than a museum or a library makes its acquisitions on the basis of nothing but popular appeal.[19]

From at least as early as 1904 until his death Barker had a vision of a national theater in England, and he worked steadfastly for its establishment. In 1904 he collaborated with William Archer on elaborate and detailed plans for such a national theater, a theater that would be the permanent home of Shakespeare and other classic English dramatists, and of translations from the great drama of other lands. The work was privately printed in that year under the title *Scheme and Estimates for a National Theatre* and published in 1907 with an endorsement by seven prominent persons in the world of the drama—Henry Irving, Squire Bancroft, James Barrie, Helen D'Oyly Carte, John Hare, Henry Arthur Jones, and Arthur Wing Pinero.[20] But the national theater was not established.

The plans of Archer and Barker are complete in every detail. The organization would be governed by a board of trustees of fifteen members. The officers and all of the employees needed (down to the cleaning women) are enumerated, along with their suggested salaries. A complete three-months' repertory of plays in a possible order of presentation is formulated. The size of the theater is given as between fifteen hundred and fifty and sixteen hundred. The prices of the tickets are suggested and even a model application form for subscription seats is provided. The plan requires a donor or donors to provide a site for the theater and guarantees for absorbing the expenses for a certain number of years at the beginning, should the enterprise not immediately pay its own way. But the authors maintain that, free from taxes and rents, the theater must be able to pay its own way and even make a profit, out of which the initial gifts would be repaid.[21]

The authors make clear that this national theater is not meant to be a pioneer theater with experiment as its primary function.[22] For this reason they omit from their specimen repertory the names of Tolstoy, Gorky, Ibsen, Hauptmann, D'Annunzio, and Shaw.[23] In a preface to the 1907 and 1908 editions of the *Scheme*, Barker states that now he would unquestionably include in the repertory all these dramatists excluded in 1904.[24] This reflection of a change in the general acceptability of these writers is probably some indication of the influence of the Vedrenne-Barker seasons at the Court Theatre between 1904 and 1907.

In 1930, Archer having died and the national theater still not having become a reality, Barker wrote another work revising the original scheme for such a project and explaining once more the need for such an organization. Circumstances had changed enough—especially the costs of such an enterprise—that some revisions in the plan and new estimates were necessary. Basically the plan is the same as the older one and equally detailed. This time, however, two auditoriums are envisioned, a large one seating eighteen to nineteen hundred and a small one seating a thousand to eleven hundred.[25] Although the theater would present classics regularly (out of forty-nine plays suggested for the first season twelve are Shakespeare's),[26] now an important function of the theater would be the cultivation of new dramatists. The financing of the theater, no benevolent millionaire having been discovered to donate the three hundred and fifty thousand pounds needed in 1904,[27] Barker thought could come from a portion of the funds the government earned from licensing radio sets.[28] In 1930 the estimated total initial cost of the undertaking was almost three times the earlier figure, or one million pounds.[29]

These two complete and detailed schemes not only illustrate Barker's practical knowledge of the theater but also are convincing evidence that he was sincerely enough interested in bringing into existence a national theater to work hard for it. He saw such a theater as having numerous important functions: it would preserve plays in their living form on the stage; it would encourage the neglected art of acting, not in individual virtuoso performances but in cooperative effort; it would help to develop new dramatists; it would raise the expectations of audiences, who then in turn would demand and encourage improvements in drama and acting.[30]

Unfortunately Barker's plan did not become a reality during his lifetime. In 1945 in *The Use of the Drama* he was still forced to comment on the commercialism of the theater, and on the danger of the drama becoming simply part of a mammoth entertainment industry which determines the success or failure of a play on the basis of financial return.[31] One is reminded of the bleak prophecy in *The Harlequinade* of the mechanical theater of the future for which play-making factories turn out material endlessly.

Undoubtedly Barker would have been gratified at the final establishment of the National Theatre in England in 1963 with the Old Vic as its home, and even more pleased at its moving in 1976 to its splendid new structure on the South Bank of the Thames. The National Theatre complex has three auditoriums: the open stage Olivier, with eleven hundred and sixty seats; the proscenium stage Lyttleton, with eight hundred and ninety seats; and the experimental Cottesloe, with four hundred seats. It has an annual government subsidy of five million dollars. In many respects it shows the influence of suggestions made earlier by Barker.

In addition to his comments on the place of the drama in society, the relationship among the dramatist, the actor, and the audience, and the need for a national home for great plays, throughout Barker's critical writings are found perceptive remarks about individual authors and plays. In his book *On Dramatic Method*, for example, he shows a comprehensive knowledge of the drama from the time of the Greeks to his own day as he discusses its development mainly from the technical point of view, considering topics such as the unities, the use of blank verse and rhyme, various types of staging, and conventions in the drama. Although he wrote more on Shakespeare than on any other playwright, yet his comments on others are also of value in themselves and in throwing light on Barker's basic attitudes.

There are, says Barker, two methods of playwriting—the explicit and the implicit. In the former the words and action reveal the meaning fairly directly; in the latter much of the meaning is indirectly expressed between the lines. The actors must make it clear not by what they say and do but through the contribution of their presence and their contrasting attitudes. Barker classifies Marlowe's plays as entirely explicit. Shakespeare's earlier plays also belong in this category, and this is his general method so far as possible. Bernard Shaw is explicit, too. But modern drama makes much use of the implicit method—Chekhov, for example, and sometimes Ibsen, Maeterlinck, and Yeats.[32] And, one might add, Barker himself. Chekhov's plays more than any others call for the collaboration of the actor; "they are *libretti* waiting for music." There is immense subtlety in them, and their construction is a technical triumph, but for them to be successfully presented an understanding of the characters and of Russian life is absolutely essential.[33]

Barker contrasts Shavian drama in general with Chekhov's. Shaw's plays demand more ability in rhetorical speech, but there can scarcely be any argument about their interpretation, for very little is left unsaid. Is one method of playwriting necessarily better than the other? No, says Barker, for both can result in good plays. But Chekhov's require more of the actor and therefore, well done, may be more satisfying. On the other hand, if not properly performed, Chekhov's can be incomprehensible, whereas Shaw's meaning is always clear.[34]

Naturally Barker, having been involved in the "new drama" himself, has admiration for Ibsen. He presents in *The Use of the Drama* an excellent analysis of Ibsen's *Rosmersholm*, which he praises highly. It illustrates, he says, the "artist and craftsman combined." Ibsen presents the tragic story of Rosmer and Rebecca in two hours of overheard conversation ("a masterpiece of condensation"), very nearly as it might happen in life. The dialogue is used for several purposes at the same time. It propels the action; it characterizes the speakers, the listeners, and others as well; and it paints a picture of Rosmersholm itself. The characters seem to have lives of their own, apart from the author. Moreover, although there is little action, the revelations about human nature are exciting.[35]

In *On Dramatic Method* Barker insists that Ibsen is a poet whether he writes in verse or prose. Ibsen succeeds in coordinating sense and sound—even in translations this is apparent, and in giving to seemingly everyday speech the powerful emotional effect of poetry.[36] He recognizes that the drama of the inner life may be as strong as any outward conflict. So he gives us the drama of mind and spirit.[37] It is "a drama rather of being than doing" which results from Ibsen's method of retrospection with its emphasis on the unfolding of character.[38]

Barker calls Ibsen "the great dramatic economist." Although short, his plays need to be so because they are so intense in their mixture of thought and emotion.[39] Indeed he suggests that Swinburne's fifteen thousand line *Bothwell* (almost four times the length of *Hamlet*) and Shaw's *Back to Methuselah* might have been better plays if their authors had pruned them to a more manageable length.[40] A good example of Ibsen's economy of means Barker finds to be the very opening of *Rosmersholm*, with Rebecca sitting crocheting *"a large white woollen shawl which is nearly finished."* Crocheting, he points out, is done by one who sits thinking, waiting; the fact that she has nearly finished a large shawl shows that she has been doing it for a long time.[41]

This comment on a stage direction reminds one of Barker's own stage directions, in which each detail also has significance. And his admiration of Ibsen's drama of the inner life is what one might expect from the man whose own plays (*The Secret Life*, for example) show similar characteristics.

Barker's sympathy in his criticism as in his plays is not completely with the limitations of realistic drama. Realism is, after all, he recognizes, a convention like any other. He commends Barrie's attempt "to wed fancy and poetry to the actualities of his realistic modern stage," which, even though it did not win him complete freedom, did pave the way for others.[42] He praises Maeterlinck's use of symbolism in his *Three Plays* (*Alladine and Palomides*, *Interior*, and *The Death of Tintagiles*) as "the only way of saying much in little," but cautions against any attempt to work out the symbolism of these plays with mathematical exactness. Though Maeterlinck calls them "little dramas for marionettes," these are "real plays," insists Barker. They might not be successful in the contemporary theater (of 1910), but that is the theater's fault, not theirs.[43] He makes the same statement about Laurence Housman's *Little Plays of St. Francis* in his preface to that work.[44] The elements of fantasy and symbolism which appear in Barker's own plays he thus praises in the work of other playwrights.

Barker's *On Poetry in Drama* shows his sympathy toward this medium of expression. He credits Maeterlinck and Yeats with beginning the revival of poetic drama. Though Maeterlinck wrote in prose, Barker nevertheless calls him a poet because he is concerned with that which is beneath surface appearances.[45] He praises O'Casey, Eliot, and Auden for trying to break loose from the restrictions of the realistic theater, which he feels may be losing its vitality.

He warns the poet-dramatists, however, that they must pay attention to more than mere form; they must learn that the most important element in the drama is the creation of convincing characters who will have a life of their own beyond their representation by actors. Although he observes that the playwright first thinks of his play in relation to action, as he matures he grows to emphasize character, and the relations of the characters to one another. "Great plays," says Barker, "will always, I think, be found to be balanced constructions of character."[47]

The only proper medium of expression for this sort of characterization, Barker believes, is poetry, by which he means economical, emotional language, be it verse or prose. Drama requires a language capable of expressing thought and feeling together, and at times almost feeling alone, a language which will appeal in subtle, nonrational ways, and which will be economical, suggestive, and striking.[48] Thus poetry and drama are very closely allied. Though a good poet is not necessarily a good dramatist, "what great dramatist," asks Barker, "has not been a poet?"[49]

The greatest of these dramatist-poets, of course, is Shakespeare, and about him Barker has a great deal to say. For most readers and students of the drama probably the most popular and valuable of Barker's critical works is and will continue to be his *Prefaces to Shakespeare*. Barker's interest in Shakespeare began early in his acting career, his first big success being his performance as Richard II; it was further evidenced in his own productions of *Twelfth Night* and *A Winter's Tale* at the Savoy and of *A Midsummer Night's Dream* in both London and New York; and it reached its climax with the series of *Prefaces*. The first prefaces were published with acting editions of the three plays he produced at the Savoy. Then came a number of them originally commissioned as contributions to an edition called *The Players' Shakespeare*, of which only seven volumes were published, each containing one play. The prefaces to these plays—*Macbeth*, *The Merchant of Venice*, *Cymbeline*, *A Midsummer Night's Dream*, *Love's Labour's Lost*, *Julius Caesar*, and *King Lear*—were also published separately. Although *The Players' Shakespeare* series was never completed, Barker went on with his work, expanding it beyond the original dimensions.[50] Five series of *Prefaces* were published separately, and later (in 1946—47) combined in a two-volume edition which incorporates some revisions. In them Barker comments on ten plays: *Hamlet*, *King Lear*, *The Merchant of Venice*, *Antony and Cleopatra*, *Cymbeline*, *Othello*, *Coriolanus*, *Romeo and Juliet*, *Julius Caesar*, and *Love's Labour's Lost*. They vary considerably in length, from thirty-two pages for *The Merchant of Venice* to two hundred and thirty-seven for *Hamlet*. In 1974 another volume was published, titled *More Prefaces to Shakespeare*, which contains the original prefaces to the acting editions of *Twelfth Night*, *A Winter's Tale*, and *A Midsummer Night's Dream*; the introduction and the prefaces to *The Players' Shakespeare* editions of *Macbeth* and *A Midsummer Night's Dream*; and the long critical essay "From *Henry V* to *Hamlet*."

Barker's fundamental attitude toward Shakespeare is that he was a master playwright, a stage craftsman, who was writing for a certain type of theater, the conditions of which determined to a great extent the way in which he wrote. We must understand these conditions in order to interpret the plays as Shakespeare intended them to be done. To Barker, unlike William Poel, however, this does not mean performing them on a reproduction of the Elizabethan stage, but trying to achieve the same effects by the means available to us.[51]

In this attempt to understand Shakespeare's plays, Barker combines the capacities of the scholar and the man of the theater. He has a wide knowledge of Shakespearian scholarship. He pays tribute to the work of Dr. A. W. Pollard and Sir Edmund Chambers; he has studied the original texts of the plays as well as the work of later editors; he refers to the comments of critics like Dr. Johnson, Charles Lamb, Edward Dowden, A. C. Bradley, and Dover Wilson when there is reason to. But Barker is not merely the scholar who has pored over Shakespeare in his study and thought of him as a poet who happened to write in dramatic form. He is an experienced man of the theater himself, and it is his approach to the plays as first of all works meant to be performed by actors in a theater and his capabilities in pursuing this approach that give special importance to the prefaces.

Barker's insistence that closet drama is an anomaly and that a play is not fully realized except in the presentation of it by actors upon a stage is reiterated in the case of Shakespeare. There must be a collaboration between the dramatist and the actor. "The text of a play is a score waiting performance . . . ," he once agains states.[52] Even the most difficult to stage of all the plays, *King Lear*, is to Barker first of all a play. Shakespeare meant it to be acted; it was acted; it can be acted. Barker begins the preface to *Lear* by quoting Charles Lamb's famous dictum "Lear is essentially impossible to be represented on a stage," and explains that he will attempt to prove the contrary. He disagrees with Bradley's opinion that performance ruins the storm scenes. Even if we admit the remote possibility that Shakespeare's genius might just this once have impelled him to write an unactable play, Barker maintains that the actors and the audience of his day were not aware of the fact. Moreover, he protests that Shakespeare, rather than failing, has "triumphantly succeeded," if we consider the play in terms of the Elizabethan stage.[53]

Barker's understanding of Elizabethan stagecraft is certainly as thorough as is possible with our knowledge of the Elizabethan theater. Shakespeare's was not a realistic method of presentation, he points out, in the modern sense of having scenery painted to resemble the actual world, costumes historically accurate, dialogue written and spoken to suggest ordinary conversation. Shakespeare was forced to conform to the limitations of his theater, but, Barker constantly indicates, these "limitations" were turned by the master dramatist to advantages. The storm scenes in *Lear*, for example, cannot be successfully presented in a realistic fashion. Instead of trying to provide through the mechanical means available in the modern theater a storm that would rival and quite possibly overwhelm the actor, however, the producer today would do better to follow Shakespeare in associating the storm with the man. He has the actor "impersonate both Lear and —reflected in Lear—the storm." He creates the storm through the medium of dramatic poetry. No reasonable actor, says Barker, would try to act the scenes realistically.[54] Barker presents his argument in a thorough fashion and with the weight of his experience behind it, it is convincing.

Barker gives much attention to the fact that because the Elizabethan stage was unlocalized and there was no elaborate physical production, Shakespeare was able to make the most of contrasts between characters and scenes, contrasts which later scenic productions destroy at the same time as they lengthen the time of performance. Only on an unlocalized stage do these contrasts acquire their full value.

For example, in *Romeo and Juliet* Capulet and Paris plan Juliet's marriage to Paris on the outer stage. Immediately following their departure, Romeo and Juliet appear after their wedding night at the window above, unaware of the complication which the audience knows has been created.[55] This sort of contrast Barker finds Shakespeare using time and again, and, he emphasizes, it is not possible if there must be waits for scene changing. The rapid shifting of locale in *Antony and Cleopatra*, too, is not possible in a modern production with elaborate scenery. Barker comments on the fact that acts 3 and 4 consist of twenty-eight scenes which editors have carefully labeled with localities, and on the basis of this localization they have then decided that Shakespeare is shifting scenes too rapidly. But Shakespeare did not localize the scenes, with the result that properly presented it is the characters, not the settings, which hold the audience's interest. Indeed for Shakespeare no locales had any reality of their own. The bare stage could serve as whatever place was needed, or not be identified as any particular locale.[56]

Another convention of the Elizabethan theater which Barker discusses in relation to its effect on Shakespeare's work is the acting of women's parts by boys. Here again, Barker shows, Shakespeare did not find this a limitation, as we might think, but an advantage. He does not present scenes of physical lovemaking, which might not have been successful under the circumstances, either in *Romeo and Juliet*, for example, or in *Antony and Cleopatra*, but rather he elevates the love scenes to an intellectual and spiritual plane, which adds to their power and results in admirable portrayals of women. Cleopatra, for instance, is not given a single scene in which to show her sensual attraction for Antony, though she reveals it in her speech when he is not on stage, and though Enobarbus describes her charms to us. She and Antony are never shown alone together. Instead of making capital of feminine sex appeal, then, as a modern dramatist might, Shakespeare must perforce "endow her with other charms for conquest: wit, coquetry, perception, subtlety, imagination, inconsequence. . . ." And, asks Barker, "How does a Cleopatra differ from the common run of wantons but in just such gifts as these? It would take a commonplace dramatist to insist upon the obvious, upon all that age does wither, while custom even sooner stales its infinite monotony!"[57]

In his analysis of Shakespeare's use of the convention of time, Barker shows that to Shakespeare it is only dramatic time that matters, not clock or calendar time. The "ambiguity of time" in *Othello*, for example, is necessary for the dramatic effect. From one point of view the action is rushed to such a degree that Desdemona would not have had time to commit adultery with Cassio. This hastening of the action is necessary, explains Barker, for were Othello given time to think or to question anyone other than Iago he would discover Iago's treachery. Yet with his choice of words and phrases in the speeches Shakespeare at the same time creates the feeling that much more time has elapsed since the marriage so that Desdemona might indeed have had an opportunity to be unfaithful. He makes the most of both time schemes, and when we see the play we accept it with no hesitation.[58]

In *The Merchant of Venice*, too, time is treated with similar freedom. Shakespeare could have tried to synchronize the time element in the two plots. The months necessary for the forfeiture of the bond could have been matched by an equal lapse of time in the casket story, but the latter is so delicate that it cannot be stretched out. So what Shakespeare does is merely to give us an impression of time passing, without bothering to be precise and consistent.[59]

Barker's general plan in these *Prefaces* is first to describe the construction and action of the play in considerable detail, telling the story with a liberal use of quotations and elucidating the effects created by Shakespeare. Then he comments on topics such as act division, the verse and prose, the costuming and scenery, and, most importantly, the characters.

Shakespeare's drama depends, with its bare stage, entirely upon its actors, Barker maintains.[60] As he goes through each of the plays, he makes suggestions to actors about how certain scenes should be played and certain lines spoken to create the desired effect, and where the very lack of speech is significant. These suggestions should be of help to the actor, and they certainly help the reader imagine the play in performance. For example, there is the scene in which the mad Lear, the blind Gloucester, and the disguised Edgar are together. Lear states that Gloucester's bastard son was kinder to his father than his lawful daughters were to him. Gloucester realizes the hopelessness of trying to explain the true situation to the mad Lear. So Barker suggests that Gloucester here might unconsciously glance toward the stranger nearby (the disguised Edgar) and that Edgar might respond with a gesture, thus bringing out "the irony and the pathos" of the situation.[61] In *Hamlet* Barker proposes that when Hamlet asks Laertes's pardon at the end before the fencing match, Laertes's remark about his honor needing satisfaction can be made significant by having him and Claudius exchange a look that will show that they have thought up this reply together.[62] It must be admitted that some of these elucidations by Barker are so subtle that one wonders if an audience could possibly appreciate their significance. But Barker himself believes that the complete detailed effect of every play cannot be expected to be apprehended in one hearing. Like great music, it may require two or three hearings to be appreciated.[63]

With respect to act divisions Barker recognizes that we do not know what the practice was in Shakespeare's theater and that certainly the breaks made by editors are not a reliable indication of what was actually done. So he makes his own suggestions as to where pauses should come from the point of view of theatrical effect. Speed of presentation and the elimination of unnecessary breaks are what he stresses. He would achieve this speed in modern productions, as he did in his own presentations of Shakespeare, by simplicity in staging and by rapidity in speaking the verse, not by cutting lines. He does think that a few of the more vulgar jokes can be cut because they do not affect an audience of today as they did Shakespeare's and probably would not be understood. Some of the meaningless topical allusions can likewise be omitted. On the whole, however, he affirms that the plays should be left as Shakespeare wrote them.[64]

In his comments on the language of the plays Barker shows a deep understanding of the effects created through rhythm and melody and the sounds of words, but he makes almost no remarks about imagery—perhaps because it is not the element of language with which an actor would be most concerned and because Shakespearean criticism had not yet begun to concentrate on it.

Costuming and scenery he treats when there is some special need for discussion of them. His general attitude is that the decoration must in no way distract from the hearing of Shakespeare's lines; it must never vie for attention with the actors, who are "the sole interpreters Shakespeare has licensed." We know more about historical accuracy in costuming than did Shakespeare, but, says Barker, it is not up to us to correct his errors. Though Cleopatra's attire may be given some Egyptian characteristics, it still must have laces to cut unless we are to be untrue to Shakespeare, for he knows how to convey meanings to us by such little touches as the "Cut my lace, Charmian." These must not be spoiled by mere historical accuracy in costuming.[65]

In his discussion of Shakespeare's characters, Barker recognizes that Shakespeare's presentation of character is variously influenced by external circumstances such as his sources and the convention of the boy-actress. He serves as a beneficial antidote to the romantic critics whom he chides for forgetting that these men and women are but persons in a play and not real human beings. He criticizes Bradley, for example, albeit gently and only in a footnote, for his practice of treating Shakespeare's characters like real people instead of fictional creations because it leads him to ignore technical considerations.[66] Yet Barker himself in his analyses of the characters does not altogether avoid this same manner. Of Iago, for instance, he says that the soliloquies do not reveal to us what Iago truly is, for "less than another can the man who lives by deceiving others know the truth about himself."[67] This would seem to come close to treating the character as if he were a live human being. And of Hamlet he asks, "His troubles apart, what sort of man is Hamlet?" and then proceeds to analyze his nature.[68]

The truth of the matter is, as Barker points out, that some characters are mere utility characters, while others come to life.[69] In the earlier plays characters tend to serve the requirements of the plot, although even then some of them achieve vitality. Shylock, for example, says Barker, is real from his first speech on, but the later Shakespeare might have made him more highly individualized.[70]

Barker's analyses of the characters are thus not in any sense restricted by his emphasis on these as plays designed for a certain kind of theater and influenced by that theater's requirements. He takes what Shakespeare has given us in the play and by putting together the pieces unites the complexities of the great figures (and the implications of even the minor ones) into a whole. For Barker believes—and surely he is right—that character is the focus of all great drama, not character simply as a person might reveal himself to the outside world, but the inner man.[71] The great characters in Shakespeare have achieved a life of their own, "something very like an immortal soul,"[72] a spiritual reality which Barker elsewhere says will cause a character to "transcend the actor's incarnation of it" and which "may survive the incarnation in a thousand actors."[73] It is this final spiritual reality which Barker, too, like the earlier Shakespearean critics, discusses, as well as the practical presentation of the character in the theater. But Barker's knowledge of the theater of Shakespeare's time and of his own day, and his understanding of the art of the actor in all times and theaters are what enable him to interpret Shakespeare's intentions in his character portrayal with unusual insight.

Although Barker admires Shakespeare as a dramatist and constantly points out examples of his technical mastery, poetic powers, and genius at characterization, he is nevertheless not an idolater of the great dramatist. He does not attempt to rationalize away all flaws in the plays nor does he follow the example of an earlier critic, as with

Cymbeline, and assign them all to an unknown collaborator.[74] He indicates in various places that Shakespeare might have done better than he has. For example, he criticizes the last part of *Romeo and Juliet* as poorly written.[75] He says, "Claudius does not come quite unquestionably to life."[76] Laertes's rebellion he finds not very believable.[77] And Hamlet he describes as the result of Shakespeare's failure to coordinate the character he created with the hero of his source.[78]

Barker's overall critical estimate of Shakespeare is, of course, very high, and it is an estimate based on Shakespeare not as a thinker or even as a poet, but as a dramatist. Shakespeare's is not the greatest intellect and others have written equally good poetry, suggests Barker, but as a dramatist he is without peer.[79]

Although the *Prefaces* cannot give us the stage productions themselves, they do, as one reviewer has said, bring us to rehearsal and place us "under the spell of the next best to Shakespeare himself."[80] When John Gielgud talked with Barker shortly before his death and urged him to return to theatrical work, Barker responded that he felt that his writing was more important. The written word could be of permanent help to actors, producers, and scholars, whereas preparing a play for a performance of "inevitable imperfection" was of no lasting value.[81] Indeed the *Prefaces* are Barker's own productions in words of Shakespeare's plays—careful, scholarly, and at the same time imaginative, poetic, and based on practical knowledge of the theater. On the whole, they are absorbing and even exciting.

Interesting, original, and searching though they are, the *Prefaces* are not always easy reading. The great amount of detail, the extensive use of quotations, and the broken-up sentence structure demand close attention. One of Barker's favorite devices, not only in the *Prefaces* but generally in his critical work, is the use of long parenthetical elements which can be confusing, as here: "And she has primed herself—clearly she does not relish the task; the subject is a ticklish one; it is Claudius, she announces, who is offended—to be 'round with him.' "[82] On the other hand, though he is serious most of the time, he does occasionally reveal a sense of humor and a felicity in expression, as in the description of Cleopatra already quoted (on page 128).

Barker's *Prefaces* are of such importance that it seems impossible that any producer of Shakespeare would now start his work without having studied them in detail. Undoubtedly they have been consulted by producers and have influenced modern presentations of Shakespeare. For instance, John Gielgud tells us that Harcourt Williams as director of the Old Vic based four productions on Barker's *Prefaces* during the 1929–30 seasons—*Romeo and Juliet*, *Antony and Cleopatra*, *King Lear*, and *The Merchant of Venice*.[83] Tyrone Guthrie, too, was familiar with the *Prefaces* and decided in 1933–34 at the Old Vic to do Shakespeare in Barker's style with a permanent "structure," no pauses for scene changes, and fidelity to the text.[84] Margaret Webster pays tribute to Barker in a review of volume 1 of the American edition of the *Prefaces*. Says Miss Webster: "Much of Granville-Barker's thinking has already passed into common theatre practice. His reiterated insistence on the uncluttered freedom of the Elizabethan stage has already had its effect. . . . We already owe him more than we know. The present writer is glad to acknowledge a profound debt to Harley Granville-Barker. . . ."[85] Speed in performance achieved through the use of simple basic sets and at least reasonable fidelity to the original texts are indeed virtues regularly expected in Shakespearean productions today, and for this much of the credit rightly goes to Barker. Although his ideas have not always been completely and universally followed by later producers, about his pervading influence no doubt exists.

The *Prefaces to Shakespeare* round out Barker's lifetime of work in and for the theater. His critical writings are a clear reflection of the same ideas and ideals revealed in the other phases of his activity. A recognition of the importance of the contribution of the actor to the full realization of the play is perhaps not unexpected from one who has been an actor himself. The understanding of the importance of characterization in drama, of being rather than outward action, of coordinated teamwork rather than star performances, and of subtle detail suggests the nature of Barker's productions and of his own plays. His sympathy with nonrealistic drama is in keeping with the quality of fantasy and symbolism in some of his own work. His intensity of purpose with regard to the place of drama in a nation's life and the need for a national theater is an extension of his own attempts to produce new noncommercial plays and a reflection of the serious intellectual character of much of his dramatic work. His Shakespeare productions were an earlier indication than the *Prefaces* of his ideas on how the plays should be presented.

Thus Barker's work in and for the theater is all interrelated and unified. It shows an intelligent, serious, idealistic personality; it is the work of a man of many and great abilities. His accomplishments as a producer, a dramatist, and a critic are of lasting importance and insure Granville Barker a permanent place in the history of English drama.

Notes and References

Preface

1. Bernard Shaw, "Barker's Wild Oats," *Harper's*, January 1947, p. 52.

Chapter One

1. Unpublished letter to the author from Shaw, July 8, 1950. Barker adopted the hyphenated form of his name (Granville-Barker) in 1918. For the sake of consistency and simplicity the original form is used in this book except in quotations.

2. The best concise biographical sketch of Barker is in Margery M. Morgan, *A Drama of Political Man: A Study in the Plays of Harley Granville Barker* (London, 1961). The only book-length biography is C. B. Purdom's *Granville Barker: Man of the Theatre, Dramatist and Scholar* (Cambridge, Mass., 1956). I am indebted especially to the latter for information used in this book.

3. Shaw, pp. 49−50.

4. Desmond MacCarthy, *The Court Theatre 1904−1907: A Commentary and Criticism*, ed. Stanley Weintraub (Coral Gables, Fla., 1966), p. 66.

5. Ibid., p. 18.

6. Ibid., pp. 111−46 (reprints the Court Theatre programs).

7. Ibid., p. 75.

8. Geoffrey Whitworth, *Harley Granville-Barker 1877−1946* (London, 1948), p. 9.

9. Review of *Man and Superman*, in *Drama and Life* (New York: Brentano's, 1908), p. 232.

10. MacCarthy, p. 88.

11. Ibid., p. 70.

12. Hesketh Pearson, *G.B.S.: A Postscript* (New York, 1950), p. 51.

13. MacCarthy, pp. 38−39.

14. Ibid., p. 81.

15. Whitworth, p. 9.

16. Max Beerbohm, *Around Theatres* (New York: A. A. Knopf, 1930), 2: 602.

17. Letter from Shaw.

18. Beerbohm, 2: 602.

19. Frank A. Swinnerton, *The Georgian Scene: A Literary Panorama* (New York: Farrar and Rinehart, 1934), p. 214.

20. Ignotus, "Mr. Granville Barker," *Spectator*, March 28, 1908, p. 500.

21. Felix Aylmer, "One That Got Away," *Drama*, n.s. no. 86 (Autumn 1967), p. 32.

22. Shaw, p. 52.

23. Pearson, *G.B.S.: A Postscript*, p. 85.

24. Swinnerton, p. 217.

25. Obituary Notice, *Drama*, n.s. no. 3 (Winter 1946), p. 3.

Chapter Two

1. Mario Borsa, *The English Stage of Today* (London: John Lane, 1908), pp. 99—102.

2. Archibald Henderson, *European Dramatists* (Cincinnati, 1913), pp. 369—70.

3. Hesketh Pearson, *Modern Men and Mummers* (New York, 1922), p. 169.

4. MacCarthy, p. 11.

5. Shaw, p. 50.

6. MacCarthy, p. 108.

7. Letter from Shaw.

8. MacCarthy, p. 108.

9. Ibid., pp. 23—25.

10. Shaw, p. 53.

11. St. John Ervine, *The Theatre in My Time* (London: Rich and Cowan, 1933), p. 38.

12. Pearson, *G.B.S.: A Postscript*, p. 53.

13. Ibid., p. 52.

14. Ignotus, pp. 499—500.

15. Borsa, pp. 112—13.

16. Whitworth, pp. 9—10.

17. Pearson, *Modern Men and Mummers*, p. 167.

18. MacCarthy, p. 43.

19. Mrs. Patrick Campbell, *My Life and Some Letters* (New York: Dodd, Mead, and Co., 1922), pp. 275—76.

20. Unpublished letter to the author from Walter Hampden, July 10, 1950.

21. Letter from Shaw.

22. Pearson, *Modern Men and Mummers*, pp. 167—68.

23. Pearson, *G.B.S.: A Postscript*, pp. 51—52.

24. Pearson, *Modern Man and Mummers*, p. 169.

25. Shaw, p. 52.

26. Letter from Shaw.

27. MacCarthy, pp. 18—20.

28. Harrison Smith, "The Revival of Greek Tragedy in America," *Bookman* 41 (1915): 410—11.

29. *Putnam's Monthly*, September 1907, p. 768.

30. Borsa, pp. 112—13.

31. Purdom, pp. 69—82.

32. Ibid., pp. 84—85.

33. Ibid., p. 89.

34. P. P. Howe, *The Repertory Theatre: A Record and a Criticism* (London, 1910), p. 51.

35. Ibid., pp. 209—16.

36. Ibid., p. 194.

37. Anna Irene Miller, *The Independent Theatre in Europe: 1887 to the Present* (New York: Ray Long and Richard R. Smith, 1931), p. 200.

38. Purdom, pp. 119—36.

39. M. St. Clare Byrne, "Fifty Years of Shakespearian Production: 1898—1948," in *Shakespeare Survey: An Annual Survey of Shakespearian Study and Production*, vol. 2, ed. Allardyce Nicoll (Cambridge: At the University Press, 1949), pp. 1—5.

40. " 'The Winter's Tale' at the Savoy," *Spectator*, September 28, 1912, p. 450.

41. Karl Schmidt, "How Barker Puts Plays On, " *Harper's Weekly*, January 30, 1915, pp. 115—16.

42. *Blackwood's Magazine*, October 1912, p. 694.

43. Darrell Figgis, *Academy*, September 28, 1912, p. 417.

44. John Palmer, *The Future of the Theatre* (London: G. Bell and Sons, 1913), p. 60.

45. *London Times*, as quoted in Byrne, p. 7.

46. Ibid, p. 8.

47. John Palmer, *Saturday Review*, September 28, 1912, p. 391.

48. Darrell Figgis, *Academy*, September 28, 1912, p. 418.

49. *Illustrated London News*, November 23, 1912, p. 780.

50. Darrell Figgis, *Academy*, November 23, 1912, pp. 674—75.

51. Quoted in Byrne, p. 7.

52. John Palmer, *Saturday Review*, November 23, 1912, pp. 637–38.

53. John Drinkwater, *The Art of Theatre-Going* (Boston: Houghton Mifflin Co., 1927), p. 146.

54. *Academy*, February 14, 1914, p. 214.

55. *Athenaeum*, February 14, 1914, p. 239.

56. J. E. Harold Terry, *British Review* 5 (1914): 442.

57. Byrne, p. 10.

58. Tyrone Guthrie, *A Life in the Theatre* (New York: McGraw-Hill Book Co., 1959), pp. 120–21.

59. Byrne, p. 17.

60. Purdom, pp. 145–47.

61. Ibid., p. 161.

62. "The Stage Event of the Year," *Everybody's Magazine*, May 1915, pp. 652–53.

63. "Granville Barker, the New Art of the Theatre and the New Drama," *Review of Reviews* 51 (1915): 500.

64. Quoted in "New York's Excited Impressions of Granville Barker," *Current Opinion* 58 (1915): 248.

65. *Everybody's Magazine*, May 1915, p. 652.

66. Francis Hackett, "Granville Barker in New York," *New Republic*, January 30, 1915, p. 25.

67. Lawrence Gilman, "The Advent of Mr. Granville Barker," *North American Review* 201 (1915): 440.

68. Ibid., p. 439.

69. Hackett, p. 25.

70. "Granville Barker, the New Art of the Theatre and the New Drama," p. 499.

71. *New York Times*, March 27, 1915, p. 11, col. 1.

72. Lawrence Gilman, "Shakespeare in the New Manner," *North American Review* 201 (1915): 593–95.

73. Francis Hackett, "A New Shakespeare," *New Republic*, February 20, 1915, p. 78.

74. Norman Hapgood, "Mr. Barker's Dream," *Harper's Weekly*, March 6, 1915, p. 230.

75. Smith, pp. 409–15.

76. John Gielgud, *Early Stages* (New York: Macmillan Co., 1939), pp. 133–34.

77. Shaw, p. 52.

Chapter Three

1. William Archer, *The Old Drama and the New: An Essay in Re-valuation* (New York: Dodd, Mead, and Co., 1923), p. 357.

2. Barker uses two dots in this fashion in this play, *The Voysey Inheritance*, and *Waste* in the volume *Three Plays* to indicate a pause in the speech. The original versions of the plays are used throughout this book.

3. For example, Archibald Henderson, p. 381; and Frank W. Chandler, *Aspects of Modern Drama* (New York: Macmillan Co., 1914), p. 226.

4. Dixon Scott, "Mr. Granville-Barker and an Alibi," in *Men of Letters* (London: Hodder and Stoughton, 1916), p. 141.

5. Arthur E. Morgan, *Tendencies of Modern English Drama* (New York: Charles Scribner's Sons, 1924), pp. 95−96.

6. Thomas H. Dickinson, *The Contemporary Drama of England* (Boston: Little, Brown, and Co., 1931), p. 223.

7. Palmer, *The Future of the Theatre*, p. 176.

8. Graham Sutton, *Some Contemporary Dramatists* (London, 1924), p. 27.

9. Purdom, p. 307.

10. Laurence Housman, *The Unexpected Years* (Indianapolis: Bobbs-Merrill Co., 1936), p. 115.

11. Howe, p. 137.

Chapter Four

1. MacCarthy, p. 32.

2. Sutton, p. 22.

3. Henderson, pp. 384−85.

4. Archer, p. 129.

5. Edward Storer, "Dramatists of To-day," *Living Age*, January 24, 1914, p. 227.

6. Archer, pp. 357−58.

7. Ibid., p. 143.

8. Purdom, pp. 73−74.

9. Newell W. Sawyer, *The Comedy of Manners from Sheridan to Maugham* (Philadelphia: University of Pennsylvania Press, 1931), p. 115.

10. Henderson, p. 389.

11. Purdom, p. 198.

12. Ibid., pp. 245, 292.

13. Henderson, p. 390.

14. Archer, p. 360.

15. For example, J. W. Cunliffe, *English Literature in the Twentieth Century* (New York: Macmillan Co., 1933), p. 91.

16. Archer, p. 360.

17. Martin Ellehauge, *Striking Figures among Modern English Dramatists* (Copenhagen, 1931), p. 53.

18. W. L. Courtney, "Realistic Drama," *Fortnightly Review* 100 (1913): 103.

Chapter Five

1. Beginning with *The Madras House*, Barker uses three dots to indicate a pause.

2. Review of the published play, *North American Review* 195 (1912): 592–93. See also "The Younger Dramatists," *Harper's Weekly*, March 3, 1912, p. 6.

3. Harley Granville Barker, "The Theatre: The Next Phase," *English Review* 5 (1910): 648.

4. Walter Kerr, "A Treasure Revived, along with a Dud," *New York Times*, July 10, 1977, sec. D, p. 3.

5. Desmond McCarthy, review, *New Statesman*, December 5, 1925. p. 237.

6. Ludwig Lewisohn, "Concerning Granville Barker," *Nation*, November 16, 1921, p. 575.

7. Robert A. Parker, "Bernstein versus Barker," *Independent and the Weekly Review*, November 12, 1921, p. 165.

8. John van Druten, "A Quarter Century of the Rialto," *New York Times Magazine*, February 15, 1951, p. 20.

9. Ludwig Lewisohn, *The Modern Drama: An Essay in Interpretation* (New York: B. W. Huebsch, 1915), pp. 202–204.

10. MacCarthy, review, p. 238.

11. Swinnerton, p. 215.

12. The published play gives 1912 as the date of composition, but it was presented in the fall of 1911.—Purdom, p. 127.

13. Review, *Dramatist* 9 (1918): 880.

14. Clarence Britten, "Reënter Literary Burlesque," *Dial*, May 9, 1918, p. 450.

15. John Palmer, "Hors D'Oeuvres at the S. James," *Saturday Review*, September 6, 1913, pp. 293–94.

16. Leonard Inkster, "The Romantic Mr. Barker," *Saturday Review*, October 4, 1913, p. 426.

17. Harley Granville Barker, " 'The Harlequinade,' " *Saturday Review*, October 11, 1913, p. 459.

18. Dion Clayton Calthrop, *Punch and Judy: A Corner in the History of Entertainment* (London: Dubau and Co., 1926).

19. Robert Benchley, "Remnants," *Life*, July 7, 1921, p. 18.

Chapter Six

1. Margery Morgan, Introduction to *The Madras House* (London, 1977), p. xxiv.

2. Edward Shanks, "Mr. Granville-Barker's New Play," *Outlook* (London), September 15, 1923, p. 211.

3. Sutton, p. 33.

4. Ibid., p. 37.

5. Ibid., p. 38.

6. Harley Granville Barker, Introduction to *Three Plays* by Maurice Maeterlinck (London, 1911), p. vii.

7. Allardyce Nicoll, *British Drama: An Historical Survey from the Beginnings to the Present Time*, 3d ed. rev. (London: George G. Harrap and Co., 1932), pp. 456–57.

8. W. A. Darlington, *Literature in the Theatre and Other Essays* (London: Chapman and Hall, 1925), p. 191.

9. Shanks, p. 211.

10. Charles Archer, *William Archer: Life, Work and Friendships* (London: George Allen and Unwin, 1931), p. 397.

11. "Awaiting Production," *Saturday Review*, January 19, 1929, p. 79.

12. Ibid., p. 80.

13. Purdom, p. 204.

Chapter Seven

1. Henderson, p. 384.

2. Bernard Shaw, Preface to *Mrs. Warren's Profession*, in *The Collected Works of Bernard Shaw*, Ayot St. Lawrence edition (New York: William H. Wise and Co., 1930), 7: 165–68.

3. Ashley Dukes, *Modern Dramatists* (Chicago: C. H. Sergel, 1912), pp. 139–40.

4. Dickinson, p. 221.

5. Margaret Haskell, "Granville Barker as Dramatist," *Drama*, 8 (1918): 291.

6. P. P. Howe, *Dramatic Portraits* (London, 1913), pp. 206–207.

7. For example, Storm Jameson, *Modern Drama in Europe* (London: W. Collins Sons and Co., 1920), pp. 176–77; and Charlton Andrews, *The Drama Today* (Philadelphia: J. B. Lippincott Co., 1913), p. 143.

8. Palmer, *Future of the Theatre*, p. 177.

9. George P. Baker, *Dramatic Technique* (Boston: Houghton Mifflin Co., 1919), p. 278.

10. Archer, p. 364.

11. Dickinson, p. 120.

12. Letter from Shaw.

13. Harold Williams, *Modern English Writers*, 3d ed. rev. (London: Sidgwick and Jackson, 1925), p. 269.

14. Letter from Shaw.

15. Ibid.

16. Shaw, p. 52.

17. Letter from Shaw.

18. Harley Granville Barker, *The Use of the Drama* (Princeton, 1945), p. 67.

19. Scott, pp. 135–36.

20. Ervine, p. 102.

Chapter Eight

1. Harley Granville Barker, *On Dramatic Method* (London, 1931), pp. 7–8.

2. Harley Granville Barker, *The Exemplary Theatre* (Boston, 1922), pp. 46–47.

3. Ibid., pp. 268–69.

4. Ibid., p. 266.

5. Ibid., pp. 99–106.

6. Ibid., pp. 113–24.

7. Ibid., pp. 125–26.

8. Barker, *Use of Drama*, pp. 90–91.

9. Ibid., pp. 28–29.

10. Barker, *Exemplary Theatre*, p. 7.

11. Ibid., p. 126.

12. Ibid., p. 215.

13. Ibid., p. 216.

14. Ibid., p. 218.

15. Ibid., p. 233.

16. Ibid., p. 237.

17. Barker, *Use of Drama*, p. 85.

18. Barker, *Exemplary Theatre*, p. 10.

19. Barker, *Use of Drama*, pp. 66−68.

20. Published as *A National Theatre: Scheme and Estimates* (London, 1907) by William Archer and Harley Granville Barker, and as *Scheme and Estimates for a National Theatre* (New York, 1908). The endorsement comes before numbered pages.

21. Archer and Barker, *Scheme and Estimates*, p. 2.

22. Ibid., p. 36.

23. Ibid., p. 44.

24. Ibid., p. xi.

25. Harley Granville Barker, *A National Theatre* (London, 1930), p. 52.

26. Ibid., p. 70.

27. Ibid., p. vii.

28. Ibid., pp. 31−33.

29. Ibid., p. 30.

30. Ibid., pp. 9−23.

31. Barker, *Use of Drama*, p. 64.

32. Ibid., pp. 43−45.

33. Barker, *Exemplary Theatre*, pp. 130−31.

34. Ibid., pp. 124−25.

35. Barker, *Use of Drama*, pp. 53−57.

36. Barker, *On Dramatic Method*, p. 170.

37. Ibid., p. 172.

38. Ibid., p. 183.

39. Ibid., p. 169.

40. Ibid., p. 26.

41. Ibid., p. 174.

42. Harley Granville Barker, Preface to *The Boy David* by J. M. Barrie (London, 1938), p. xii.

43. Barker, Introduction to *Three Plays* by Maeterlinck, pp. vi−vii.

44. Harley Granville Barker, Preface to *Little Plays of St. Francis* by Laurence Housman, 2d ser. (London, 1931), pp. vii−viii.

45. Harley Granville Barker, *On Poetry in Drama* (London, 1937), pp. 11−12.

46. Ibid., p. 26.

47. Ibid., pp. 28−32.

48. Ibid., pp. 34−35.

49. Ibid., p. 39.

50. Author's preface to *Prefaces to Shakespeare* by Harley Granville Barker, vol. 1 (Princeton, 1946), p. v. All later references to the *Prefaces* are to this edition.

51. Ibid., 1:4.

52. Ibid., 1:5.

53. Ibid., 1:261—66.

54. Ibid., 1:266—67.

55. Harley Granville Barker, *Prefaces to Shakespeare*, vol. 2 (Princeton, 1947), pp. 315—16.

56. Barker, *Prefaces*, 1:10—11.

57. Ibid., 1:435—37.

58. Ibid., 2:24—30.

59. Ibid., 1:336—38.

60. Ibid., 1:11.

61. Ibid., 1:296.

62. Ibid., 1:211.

63. Ibid., 1:264.

64. Ibid., 1:22.

65. Ibid., 1:407—409.

66. Ibid., 2:101.

67. Ibid., 2:102.

68. Ibid., 1:244.

69. See ibid., 1:351, for example.

70. Ibid., 1:353.

71. Ibid., 1:7.

72. Ibid., 1:29.

73. Barker, *On Poetry in Drama*, pp. 30—31.

74. Barker, *Prefaces*, 1:460.

75. Ibid., 2:323.

76. Ibid., 1:223.

77. Ibid., 1:123.

78. Ibid., 1:231.

79. Ibid., 1:19—20.

80. George Rylands, review of *Prefaces to Shakespeare*, Fifth Series, *New Statesman and Nation*, February 21, 1948, p. 157.

81. John Gielgud, "Granville-Barker's Shakespeare," *Theatre Arts Monthly* 31 (October, 1947): 48—49.

82. Barker, *Prefaces*, 1:228.

83. Gielgud, "Granville-Barker's Shakespeare," p. 48.

84. Guthrie, pp. 120–21.

85. Margaret Webster, review in the *New York Times Book Review*, January 26, 1947, p. 4.

Selected Bibliography

PRIMARY SOURCES

This list includes only published material, arranged within each group in the order of first publication. A bibliography of published and unpublished works by Barker, compiled by Frederick May and Margery M. Morgan, is found in C. B. Purdom, *Harley Granville Barker* (Cambridge: Harvard University Press, 1956). I gratefully acknowledge my indebtedness to this bibliography.

I. Dramatic Works

A. Plays Written by Barker Alone

Three Plays: The Marrying of Ann Leete, The Voysey Inheritance, Waste. London: Sidgwick & Jackson, 1909; New York: Brentano's, 1909; New York: Mitchell Kennerley, 1909.

The Marrying of Ann Leete. London: Sidgwick & Jackson, 1909; Boston: Little, Brown and Co., 1916.

The Voysey Inheritance. London: Sidgwick & Jackson, 1909; rev. version. London: Sidgwick & Jackson, 1913; Boston: Little, Brown and Co., 1916; rev. version in *Plays of To-day: First Volume*. London: Sidgwick & Jackson, 1925; final version, London: Sidgwick & Jackson, 1938; Essential English Library. London: Longmans, [1959]; introduction by E. R. Wood. London: William Heinemann, 1967.

Waste. London: Sidgwick & Jackson, 1909; Boston: Little, Brown and Co., 1916; rev. version. London: Sidgwick & Jackson, 1927; rev. version in *Modern American and British Plays*, edited by S. Marion Tucker. New York: Harper and Bros., 1931.

The Madras House. London: Sidgwick & Jackson, 1911; New York: Mitchell Kennerley, 1911; Boston: Little, Brown and Co., 1916; rev. version. London: Sidgwick & Jackson, 1925; introduction and notes by Margery Morgan, reprint of 1911 version but also containing the revisions. London: Methuen, 1977.

Farewell to the Theatre. London: Sidgwick & Jackson, 1916.

Rococo and Two Others. (Vote by Ballot, Farewell to the Theatre). London: Sidgwick & Jackson, 1917.

Three Short Plays: Rococo, Vote by Ballot, Farewell to the Theatre. Boston: Little, Brown and Co., 1917.

The Secret Life. London: Chatto & Windus, 1923; London: Sidgwick & Jackson, 1923; Boston: Little, Brown and Co., 1923.

Rococo. London: Sidgwick & Jackson, 1925; New York: Samuel French, n.d.

Vote by Ballot. London: Sidgwick & Jackson, 1925.

His Majesty. London: Sidgwick & Jackson, 1928; Boston: Little, Brown and Co., 1929.

The Collected Plays of Harley Granville-Barker. Foreword by J. B. Priestley. Introductions by Ivor Brown. Vol. 1. London: Sidgwick & Jackson, 1967.

B. Plays Written in Collaboration

Prunella: or Love in a Dutch Garden, by Laurence Housman and H. Granville Barker. London: A. H. Bullen, 1906; London: Sidgwick & Jackson, 1906; New York: Brentano's, 1906; London: Sidgwick & Jackson, 1907; London: Sidgwick & Jackson, 1910; London: Sidgwick & Jackson, 1911; Boston: Little, Brown and Co., 1916; new version, with additional act (act 3). London: Sidgwick & Jackson, 1930.

The Harlequinade, by Dion Clayton Calthrop and Granville Barker. London: Sidgwick & Jackson, 1918; Boston: Little, Brown and Co., 1918.

C. English Versions of Foreign Plays

Anatol, by Arthur Schnitzler. London: Sidgwick & Jackson, 1911; New York: Mitchell Kennerley, 1911; Boston: Little, Brown and Co., 1916. Extracts from Barker's *Anatol* published as "The Little Theatre's Newest Play," *The Green Book Magazine* 8 (1912): 818–24.

Deburau, by Sacha Guitry. London: William Heinemann, 1921; London and New York: G. P. Putnam's Sons, 1921.

Doctor Knock, by Jules Romains. London: Ernest Benn, 1925; London: Sidgwick & Jackson, 1927.

Six Gentlemen in a Row, by Jules Romains. London: Sidgwick & Jackson, 1927.

D. English Versions of Spanish Plays, Written with Helen Granville-Barker

1. Plays by Gregorio Martínez Sierra
Collected Plays (The Kingdom of God, The Two Shepherds, Wife to a Famous

Man, The Romantic Young Lady). Vol. 2 of the *Plays* of Sierra. London: Chatto & Windus, 1923; New York: E. P. Dutton, [1923].

The Kingdom of God and Other Plays. Reissue of above with introduction by the translators. New York: E. P. Dutton, [1929].

The Kingdom of God. London: Sidgwick & Jackson, 1927.

The Romantic Young Lady. London: Sidgwick & Jackson, 1929.

Take Two from One. London: Sidgwick & Jackson, 1931.

The Two Shepherds. London: Sidgwick & Jackson, 1935.

2. Plays by Serafín and Joaquín Álvarez Quintero

Four Plays (The Women Have Their Way, A Hundred Years Old, Fortunato, The Lady from Alfaqueque). Introduction by the translators. London: Sidgwick & Jackson, 1927; Boston: Little, Brown and Co., 1928.

The Women Have Their Way. London: Sidgwick & Jackson, 1927.

A Hundred Years Old. London: Sidgwick & Jackson, [1927].

Fortunato. London: Sidgwick & Jackson, 1927.

The Lady from Alfaqueque. London: Sidgwick & Jackson, 1927.

Four Comedies (Love Passes By, Don Abel Wrote a Tragedy, Peace and Quiet, Doña Clarines). London: Sidgwick & Jackson, 1932; New York: Samuel French, 1932.

Love Passes By. London: Sidgwick & Jackson, [1932].

Don Abel·Wrote a Tragedy. London: Sidgwick & Jackson [1932].

Peace and Quiet. London: Sidgwick & Jackson [1932].

Doña Clarines. London: Sidgwick & Jackson [1932].

II. Critical Works by Barker

A. About Drama, Dramatists, and the Theater (Exclusive of Shakespeare)

1. Books and Lectures Published as Books or Pamphlets

Schemes and Estimates for a National Theatre, by William Archer and Granville Barker. Privately printed, 1904. The authors' names are not on the title page, but a preliminary note is signed "W. A." and "H. G. B."

A National Theatre: Scheme and Estimates, by William Archer and Granville Barker. London: Duckworth & Co., 1907. Same as preceding, with preliminary note, and letter from Granville Barker to Archer as preface. Reprint. Port Washington, N.Y.: Kennikat Press, 1970.

Scheme and Estimates for a National Theatre, by William Archer and Granville Barker. New York: Duffield & Co., 1908. Same as preceding, with additional preface to the American edition by Archer.

The Exemplary Theatre. London: Sidgwick & Jackson, 1922; Boston: Little, Brown and Co., 1922; reprint, New York: Benjamin Blom, 1969; reprint, Freeport, N.Y.: Books for Libraries Press, 1970.

A National Theatre. London: Sidgwick & Jackson, 1930.

On Dramatic Method. Being the Clark Lectures for 1930 [Trinity College, Cambridge]. London: Sidgwick & Jackson, 1931; reprint, New York: Dramabooks-Hill and Wang, 1956; reprint, London: John Calder, 1956; reprint, Toronto: Copp Clark, 1956.

The Study of Drama. A lecture given at Cambridge [England] 2 August 1934, with notes subsequently added. Cambridge: University Press, 1934. Folcroft, Pa.: Folcroft Library Editions, 1972.

On Poetry in Drama. The Romanes Lecture, delivered at the Taylor Institution, 4 June 1937. London: Sidgwick & Jackson, 1937.

The Use of the Drama. Princeton Books in the Humanities, no. 5. Based on three Spencer Trask Lectures delivered at Princeton University in 1944. Princeton: Princeton University Press, 1945; reprint, New York: Russell and Russell, [1971]; London: Sidgwick & Jackson, 1946. Slightly revised from 1945 ed.

2. Articles

"Repertory Theatres." *New Quarterly* 2 (1909): 491−504.

"The Theatre: The Next Phase." *English Review* 5 (1910): 631−48. Delivered as a lecture to the Times Literary Club, June 9, 1910. Also in *Forum* 44 (1910): 159−70.

"J. M. Barrie as a Dramatist." *Bookman* (London) 39 (October, 1910): 13−21.

"The Theatre Exhibition in Berlin." From Our Special Correspondent. *London Times*, November 7, 1910, p. 16, cols. 1−2.

"The Theatre in Berlin." From a Correspondent. *London Times*, November 19, 1910, p. 6., cols. 1−2; and November 21, 1910, p. 12, cols. 3−4.

"Two German Theatres." *Fortnightly Review*, n.s. 89 (1911): 60−70.

"The Golden Thoughts of Granville Barker." *Play Pictorial* 21 (1912): iv. Letter defending his production of *Twelfth Night*. This issue also has photographs of the production.

" 'The Harlequinade.' "*Saturday Review*, October 11, 1913, p. 459. Letter replying to review of the play.

" 'Pygmalion' in Berlin." *Harper's Weekly*, April 11, 1914, pp. 14−15.

"At the Moscow Art Theatre." *Seven Arts Magazine* 2 (1917): 659−61.

"Reconstruction in the Theatre." From the Correspondent. *London Times*, February 20, 1919, p. 11, col. 4.

"Notes on Rehearsing a Play." *Drama* 1 (1919): 2—5. Also in *Theatre* 30 (1919): 142, 236.

"The School of 'The Only Possible Theatre.'" *Drama* 10 (1920): 251—53, 300—03, 347—49.

"Duse Once More." *Fortnightly Review* 118 (1922): 79—85.

" 'Max,' Mr. Granville-Barker and the National Theatre." *Drama*, n.s. no. 27 (April 1923), pp. 121—22. An open letter from Max Beerbohm and Barker's reply.

"The Heritage of the Actor." *Quarterly Review* 240 (1923): 53—73. Same, abridged, in *Actors on Acting*. Edited by T. Cole and H. K. Chinoy. New York: Crown, 1949, pp. 299—33.

"Some Tasks for Dramatic Scholarship." In *Essays by Divers Hands*. Being the Transactions of the Royal Society of Literature of the United Kingdom, n.s. 3. Edited by Frederick S. Boas. London: Humphrey Milford, 1923, pp. 17—38.

"Notes upon the Prize Design for a National Theatre." *Drama*, n.s. no. 40 (July 1924), pp. 229—33. Also published, slightly revised, as "Plans for a National Theatre." *Drama*, Special National Theatre no. (December 1929), pp. 43—46. (This issue also includes Barker's statement, on p. 38, in "Personal Opinions on the National Theatre.") Also in *Theatre Arts Monthly* 19 (1935): 635—38.

"A Village Shakespeare Stage." *Drama*, n.s. no. 43 (December, 1924), p. 257.

"A Note upon Chapters XX and XXI of *The Elizabethan Stage*." *Review of English Studies* 1 (1925): 60—71.

Review of *Designs by Inigo Jones for Masques and Plays at Court*, with introduction and notes by Percy Simpson and C. F. Bell. *Review of English Studies* 1 (1925): 231—35.

"On Translating Plays." In *Essays by Divers Hands*. Being the Transactions of the Royal Society of Literature of the United Kingdom, n.s. 5. Edited by John Drinkwater. London: Humphrey Milford, 1925, pp. 19—42.

"William Archer." *Drama* 4 (1926): 176—78, 182.

Review of *The Physical Conditions of the Elizabethan Public Play-Houses* and *Pre-Restoration Stage Studies*, by W. J. Lawrence. *Review of English Studies* 4 (1928): 229—37.

"Hints on Producing a Play." In *The Amateur Dramatic Year Book and Community Theatre Handbook, 1928—29*. London: A. C. Black, [1928], pp. 6—16.

"Tennyson, Swinburne, Meredith and the Theatre." In *The Eighteen-Seventies: Essays by Fellows of the Royal Society of Literature*. Edited by Granville Barker. Cambridge: University Press, 1929, pp. 161–91. Also New York: Macmillan, 1929.

"Three Victorians and the Theatre." *Fortnightly Review* 126 (1929): 655–72. Same as preceding, abridged and slightly revised.

"Some Victorians Afield." *Theatre Arts Monthly* 13 (1929): 256–64, 361–72. Same as "Tennyson, Swinburne, Meredith and the Theatre," abridged.

"The Future of the Comédie Française . . . A Letter to M. Copeau." *Observer*, September 1, 1919, p. 11.

"A Letter to Jacques Copeau." *Theatre Arts Monthly* 13 (1929): 753–59. Same as preceding.

"A National Theatre." *London Times*, February 10, 1930, p. 13, col. 6; p. 14, col. 1; and February 11, 1930, p. 15, col. 6; p. 16, col. 1 Extracts from *A National Theatre*, chap. 1.

"The National Theatre." *Drama* 9 (1930): 34–36.

"J. E. Vedrenne." *The Author* 40 (1930): 75.

"The Coming of Ibsen." In *The Eighteen-Eighties: Essays by Fellows of the Royal Society of Literature*. Edited by Walter de la Mare. Cambridge: University Press, 1930, pp. 159–96. Also, slightly abridged, in *Theatre Arts Monthly* 14 (1930): 866–74, 931–39.

"Exit Planché-Enter Gilbert." In *The Eighteen-Sixties: Essays by Fellows of the Royal Society of Literature*. Edited by John Drinkwater. Cambridge: Univerity Press, 1932, pp. 108–42. A slightly different version in *London Mercury* 25 (1932): 457–66, 558–73.

"Le Théâtre Britannique d'aujourd'hui." *France-Grande Bretagne*, no. 135 (April 1934), pp. 105–17.

"On Translating Greek Tragedy." In *Essays in Honour of Gilbert Murray*. Edited by J. A. K. Thompson and A. H. Toynbee. London: Allen & Unwin, 1936, pp. 237–47.

"The Canadian Theatre." *Queen's Quarterly* 43 (1936): 256–67.

"A Theatre That Might Be." *Theatre Arts Monthly* 29 (1945): 370–77. Extracts from *The Use of the Drama*.

3. Critical Introductions or Prefaces

Introduction. *Three Plays*. By Maurice Maeterlinck. Translated by Alfred Sutro and William Archer. London: Gowans and Gray, 1911, pp. v–xi.

Preface. *Little Plays of St. Francis. First Series*. By Laurence Housman. London: Sidgwick & Jackson, 1922, pp. vii–xv.

Introduction. *Plays.* By Gregorio Martínez Sierra. English versions by John
    Garrett Underhill. Vol. I. London: Chatto & Windus, 1923, pp.
    xi—xix. Also New York: E. P. Dutton, 1923. The same introduction
    is found in *The Kingdom of God and Other Plays.* By Gregorio Martínez
    Sierra. English versions by Harley and Helen Granville-Barker. New
    York: E. P. Dutton, 1929.

Introduction. *Plays.* By Leo Tolstoy. Translated by Louise and Aylmer
    Maude. Vol. 17 of the Centenary Edition of the Works of Leo Tolstoy.
    London: Humphrey Milford for the Tolstoy Society, 1928, pp.
    vii—xxii.

Preface. *Little Plays of St. Francis. Second Series.* By Laurence Housman.
    London: Sidgwick & Jackson, 1930, pp. vii—xiv.

Introduction. *The Boy David.* By J. M. Barrie. London: Peter Davies, 1938,
    pp. vii—xxxii.

See also English versions of Spanish plays.

B. About Shakespeare

1. Acting Editions of the Plays, with Short Prefaces

The Winter's Tale. London: William Heinemann, 1912; Boston: W. H.
    Baker, 1913.

Twelfth Night. London: William Heinemann, 1912; Boston: W. H.
    Baker, 1913.

A Midsummer Night's Dream. London: William Heinemann, 1914.

2. Prefaces to *The Players' Shakespeare*

In this edition each play (with its preface) was published in a separate
volume in London by Ernest Benn, who also reprinted each preface separately.

General Introduction to *The Players' Shakespeare.* In *The Tragedie of Macbeth,*
    1923, pp. ix—xxiv. Reprinted in *The Shakespeare Stage,* no. 2 (Sep-
    tember 1953). pp. 11—21.

Preface to *The Tragedie of Macbeth,* 1923, pp. xxv—lix. Reprinted sep-
    arately, 1923.

Preface to *The Merchant of Venice,* 1923, pp. ix—xxxviii. Reprinted sep-
    arately, 1923.

Preface to *The Tragedie of Cymbeline,* 1923, pp. ix—lvi. Reprinted separately,
    1923.

Preface to *A Midsummer Night's Dream*, 1924, pp. ix—liii. Reprinted separately, 1924.

Preface to *Love's Labour's Lost*, 1924, pp. vii—liv. Reprinted separately, 1924.

Preface to *The Tragedie of Julius Caesar*, 1925, pp. ix—lxxvii. Reprinted separately, 1926.

Preface to *The Tragedie of King Lear*, 1925, pp. ix—xcix. Reprinted separately, 1927.

3. *Prefaces to Shakespeare*, Collected in Book Form

Prefaces. First Series. London: Sidgwick & Jackson, 1927. Prefaces to *Love's Labour's Lost, Julius Caesar, King Lear* (revisions of prefaces to *The Players' Shakespeare*). An extract from the preface to *King Lear*, revised in 1935, is included in *Shakespeare Criticism 1919—1935*. Introduction by Anne Bradby. London: World's Classics—Oxford University Press, 1936, pp. 109—151.

Prefaces. Second Series. London: Sidgwick & Jackson,, 1930. Prefaces to *Romeo and Juliet, The Merchant of Venice, Antony and Cleopatra,* and *Cymbeline*; the first and third based on lectures delivered at University College, Aberystwyth, the second and fourth being revisions of prefaces to *The Players' Shakespeare.*

Preface. Third Series. London: Sidgwick & Jackson, 1937. Preface to *Hamlet.*

Prefaces. Fourth Series. London: Sidgwick & Jackson, 1945. Preface to *Othello*, based on lectures delivered at Harvard College, in memory of Winthrop Ames.

Prefaces. Fifth Series. London: Sidgwick & Jackson, 1947. Preface to *Coriolanus*, based on the Alexander Lectures delivered at University College, Toronto, 1942.

Prefaces to Shakespeare. 2 vols. Princeton: Princeton University Press, 1946—47. Vol. 1: introduction, prefaces to *Hamlet, King Lear, The Merchant of Venice, Antony and Cleopatra, Cymbeline*; vol. 2: prefaces to *Othello, Coriolanus, Romeo and Juliet, Julius Caesar, Love's Labour's Lost*; 2 vols. as above. London: Batsford, [1958]; foreword, illustrations, and notes by M. St. Clare Byrne. 4 vols. Princeton: Princeton University Press, 1963. Vol. 1: general introduction, preface to *Hamlet*; vol. 2: prefaces to *King Lear, Cymbeline, Julius Caesar*; vol. 3: prefaces to *Antony and Cleopatra, Coriolanus*; vol. 4: prefaces to *Love's Labour's Lost, Romeo and Juliet, The Merchant of Venice, Othello*. The texts of the prefaces are the same as in the 2 vol. ed. Also in Princeton Paperbacks, [1965]; fore-

word, illustrations, and notes by M. St. Clare Byrne. 4 vols. as above.
London: Batsford, 1963; 5 vols. London: Batsford, 1969–71. Vol.
1: preface to *Hamlet*, 1969; vol. 2: prefaces to *King Lear, Antony
and Cleopatra*, 1970; vol. 3: prefaces to *Julius Caesar, Cymbeline*, 1971;
vol. 4: prefaces to *Othello, Love's Labour's Lost*, 1969; vol. 5: prefaces
to *Romeo and Juliet, Coriolanus*, 1970; *Prefaces to Shakespeare*. 1 vol. ed.
London: Batsford, 1972. Originally published in 2 vols.
More Prefaces to Shakespeare. Edited, with introduction by Edward M. Moore.
Princeton: Princeton University Press, 1974. Also published as *Prefaces to Shakespeare*, vol. 6. London: Batsford, 1974. Contains the acting edition prefaces to *The Winter's Tale, Twelfth Night*, and *A Mid-
summer Night's Dream*; the introduction and prefaces to *Macbeth* and
A Midsummer Night's Dream from *The Player's Shakespeare*; and "From
Henry Fifth to *Hamlet*."

4. Individual Prefaces

Preface to Hamlet. New York: Dramabook-Hill & Wang, 1957; Toronto:
Copp Clark, 1957. From *Prefaces to Shakespeare*, vol. 1.
Preface to Othello. Princeton: Princeton University Press, 1958. From *Pre-
faces to Shakespeare*, vol. 2.

5. Other Books, Articles and Published Lectures Dealing with Shakespeare

"A Midsummer Night's Dream: A Preface by Granville Barker." *New York
Times*, February 21, 1915, sec. 7, p. 4, col. 6.
"A Producer's Preface on 'Twelfth Night.'" *Drama* 10 (1919): 87–90.
"From *Henry V* to *Hamlet*." British Academy Annual Shakespeare Lecture for
1925. *Proceedings of the British Academy* 11 (1924–25): 283–309;
London: Humphrey Milford for the British Academy, Oxford Uni-
versity Press, 1927; In *Aspects of Shakespeare*. Edited by J. W. Mackail.
Oxford: Clarendon Press, 1933, pp. 49–93; Folcroft, Pa.: Folcroft,
1976; Norwood, Pa.: Norwood, 1977.
"Shakespeare and Modern Stagecraft." *Yale Review* 15 (1926): 703–24.
"The Stagecraft of Shakespeare." *Fortnightly Review* 126 (1926): 1–17.
A condensed version of preceding.
"*Hamlet* in Plus Fours." *Yale Review* 16 (1926): 205. A one-paragraph
postcript to "Shakespeare and Modern Stagecraft."
"William Shakespeare 1564–1616." In *The Outline of Literature*. New York:
G. P. Putnam's Sons, 1926, 2: 299–350.
Associating with Shakespeare. An address delivered to the Shakespeare Associ-
ation, King's College, London, 25 November 1931. London:

Humphrey Milford for the Shakespeare Association, Oxford University Press, 1932; Folcroft, Pa.: Folcroft, 1974.

"Progrès du drame shakespearien." *Cahiers du Sud* 10, special number, *Le Théâtre Elizabéthain.* (Marseilles, June 1933), pp. 25—28; in *Le Théâtre Elizabéthain. Etudes et Traductions.* Edited by Georgette Camille and Pierre d'Exideuil. Marseilles: Les Cahiers du Sud, and Paris: Librairie Jose Corti, 1940, pp. 44—47.

"Shakespeare's Dramatic Art." In *A Companion to Shakespeare Studies.* See below.

A Companion to Shakespeare Studies. Edited by Harley Granville-Barker and G. B. Harrison. Cambridge: University Press, 1934; New York: Macmillan, 1934; Garden City, N.Y.: Anchor-Doubleday, 1960.

"The Casting of Hamlet: A Fragment." *London Mercury* 35 (November 1936): 10—17.

"Alas, Poor Will!" *Listener* 17 (1937): 287—89. The text of a radio broadcast.

"The Perennial Shakespeare." *Listener* 18 (1937): 823—26, 857—59. Described as the nineteenth of the Broadcast National Lectures, delivered on October 13, 1937; "The Perennial Shakespeare." London: British Broadcasting Corp., 1937. Described as the twentieth of the Broadcast National Lectures.

Review of *The Frontiers of the Drama*, by Una Ellis-Fermor. *Review of English Studies* 22 (1946): 144—47.

"Verse and Speech in *Coriolanus.*" *Review of English Studies* 23 (1947): 1—15.

III. Other Works by Barker (Not Related to the Drama or Theater)

"Georgiana," *English Review* 1 (1909): 420—31, 690—99. A short story.

Souls on Fifth. Boston: Little, Brown, 1916. A short story. Also in *Century* 91 (1916): 817—32; and *Fortnightly Review* 107 (1917): 336—47, 525—36.

"Acids in Solution." *Harper's Weekly,* January 29, 1916, pp. 107—108. Also published as "Trivialities: No. I. Acids in Solution." *English Review* 22 (1916): 129—34.

The Red Cross in France. Preface by Sir Frederick Treves. London: Hodder & Stoughton, 1916; preface by Joseph H. Choate. New York: George H. Doran, [1916].

The Eighteen-Seventies: Essays by Fellows of the Royal Society of Literature. Edited by Harley Granville-Barker. Cambridge: University Press,

1929; Great Neck, N.Y.: Core Collection Books, 1978.

"Help for 'Unpopular' Literature." *The Author* 41 (1931): 56–57. Extracts from a speech made at the Annual Dinner of the Society of Authors.

"The Spirit of France." *London Times* French number, July 19, 1938, p. iii, cols. 5–6; p. iv, cols. 1–2.

Quality. Presidential Address to the English Association. London: Humphrey Milford for the English Association, Oxford University Press, 1938; reprint, Folcroft, Pa.: Folcroft Press, 1971.

Speech at a Complimentary Dinner to Dr. C. E. Wheeler. *British Homeopathic Journal* 29 (January 1939): 65–66.

"A Pleasant Walk." *Cornhill Magazine*, April 1946, pp. 52–57.

SECONDARY SOURCES

Adams, W. Bridges. "The Lost Leader." *Listener* 50 (1953): 173–175. Reviews Barker's work as an actor and as a producer at the Court and the Savoy, and comments on his retirement to write. Praises the *Prefaces to Shakespeare* as more valuable than his actual productions. Nothing about him as a dramatist.

———. "Granville-Barker and the Savoy." *Drama* no. 52 (Spring 1959), pp. 28–31. Praises the Shakespeare productions, especially *A Winter's Tale*. Suggests we have no right to criticize Barker for giving up the theater.

Byrne, M. St. Clare. "Fifty Years of Shakespearian Production: 1898–1948." In *Shakespeare Survey: An Annual Survey of Shakespearian Study and Production*, vol. 2. Edited by Allardyce Nicoll. Cambridge: University Press, 1949, pp. 1–20. A helpful summary of Shakespeare production in this period, acknowledging the importance of Barker in the emphasis on fidelity to the text, the elimination of heavy scenery, and the rise of the producer as the artistic controller of the production.

———. Foreword and introduction to the illustrations. *Prefaces to Shakespeare*, by Harley Granville-Barker. London: Batsford, 1963. The foreword (1: vii–xxii) describes Barker's Shakespeare productions and suggests that without them the prefaces would not have been written. The introduction to the illustrations (2: xi–xlv) gives a fine summary of Shakespeare productions since Barker's, indicating how Barker's productions and prefaces have influenced them.

Cunliffe, John W. "Harley Granville-Barker." In *Modern English Playwrights: A Short History of the English Drama from 1825.* New York: Harper, 1927, pp. 114–121. Emphasizes the difficulty of presenting his plays because they are too intellectual.

Dickinson, Thomas H. *The Contemporary Drama of England.* Boston: Little, Brown, 1931, passim. Brief summary of Barker's work as a producer and as a dramatist through *The Secret Life.* Says he missed being one of the great contemporary dramatists because he lacked "the sense of conviction."

Downer, Alan S. "Harley Granville-Barker." *Sewanee Review* 55 (1947): 627–45. Mostly a highly commendatory description of Barker's Shakespeare productions and the *Prefaces*, pointing out that Barker's approach is that of the actor.

Ellehauge, Martin. *Striking Figures among Modern English Dramatists.* Copenhagen: Levin and Munksgaard, 1931, pp. 47–60. Excellent chapter discussing all the plays except *The Harlequinade*, pointing out Barker's growing spirituality and symbolism.

Evans, T. F. "Granville Barker: Shavian Disciple." *Shaw Bulletin* 2 (1958): 1–19. Admirable analysis and criticism of Barker's six full-length plays as plays of ideas. The title is misleading: the article emphasizes the differences between the two dramatists.

Haskell, Margaret. "Granville Barker as Dramatist." *Drama* 8 (1918) 284–294. Review of his plays to this date, suggesting that his forte lies in creating a social milieu, which is characteristically one of decadence.

Henderson, Archibald. *European Dramatists.* London: Appleton, 1926, pp. 371–406. A sympathetic discussion, briefly of Barker's work as actor and producer, more in detail of his plays through *The Secret Life.*

Howe, P. P. *Dramatic Portraits.* New York: Mitchell Kennerley, 1913; London: Martin Secker, 1913, pp. 185–207. Same entitled "Plays of Granville Barker." *Fortnightly Review* 100 (1913): 476–87, Enlightening comments on *The Marrying of*

Ann Leete, The Voysey Inheritance, Waste, and *The Madras House* as plays that work, analyzing the dialogue specifically, to show how naturally it reveals character.

————. *The Repertory Theatre: A Record and a Criticism.* New York: Mitchell Kennerley, 1911. Excellent account of Barker's repertory season for Charles Frohman at the Duke of York's Theatre in 1910, with preliminary chapters on "The Repertory Idea" and earlier "Experiments in Repertory," including the Vedrenne-Barker seasons at the Court. Very favorable comments on *The Madras House* and *Prunella* in the discussion of the plays produced.

Jackson, Anthony. "Harley Granville Barker as Director at the Royal Court Theatre, 1904—1907." *Theatre Research* 12 (1972): 126—38. Fine description of Barker's methods as a director, based on an interview with Lewis Casson as well as published sources.

Kauffmann, Stanley. "A Life in the Theatre." *Horizon* 17 (Autumn 1975): 80—85. Reprinted as "The Lives of Granville Barker" in Kauffmann's *Persons of the Drama: Theater Criticism and Comment* (New York: Harper and Row, 1976), pp. 317—28. Well-written combination of biographical and critical information, praising Barker's contributions in the various aspects of his career. An excellent introduction to Barker.

MacCarthy, Desmond. *The Court Theatre 1904—1907: A Commentary and Criticism.* Edited with foreword, introduction, and additional material, by Stanley Weintraub. Coral Gables, Fla: University of Miami Press, 1966. Indispensable record of the Vedrenne-Barker years at the Court, reviewing the plays and performances, with an appendix reproducing all the programs and listing the plays performed with number of performances. This edition also contains an additional appendix: "The Complimentary Dinner to Mr. J. E. Vedrenne and Mr. H. Granville Barker: A Transcript of the Proceedings," and an excellent introduction by the editor evaluating the significance of the Court Theatre venture.

Morgan, Margery M. *A Drama of Political Man: A Study in the Plays of Harley Granville Barker.* London: Sidgwick & Jackson, 1961. The only book-length study devoted to Barker's plays, both published and unpublished. Presents a very favorable and exhaustive analysis of them, including interesting (if sometimes rather strained) observations about their imagery and style.

Morgan, Margery M. and May, Frederick. "The Early Plays of Harley Granville Barker." *Modern Language Review* 51 (1956): 324—38. Gives an account of Barker's meeting with and collaboration with Berte Thomas. Summarizes and comments in some detail on three collaborations: "The Family of the Oldroyds," "The Weather-hen," and "Our Visitor to 'Work-a-Day.'" Corrects some details in Purdom's biography (q.v.).

Pearson, Hesketh. *G.B.S.: A Postscript*. New York: Harper, 1950. Quotes Shaw on his relationship with the second Mrs. Barker, describes Barker's methods as a producer, accuses Barker of losing sight of Shakespeare the man in his *Prefaces*.

————. *The Last Actor-Managers*. New York: Harper, 1950, pp. 71—79. A brief, not entirely sympathetic, review of Barker's career as an actor and a producer.

————. *Modern Men and Mummers*. New York: Harcourt, Brace, 1922, pp. 161—70. Calls Barker "the greatest producer of his time in England"; describes his manner of showing annoyance at rehearsals and his expectation that the actor suggest things in his portrayal that cannot be suggested.

Purdom, C. B. *Harley Granville Barker: Man of the Theatre, Dramatist, and Scholar*. Cambridge: Harvard University Press, 1956; reprint ed., Westford, Conn.: Greenwood Press, 1971; reprint ed., Philadelphia: Richard West, 1975. The only book-length biography of Barker, containing much valuable factual material about his ancestry, his life, and his work as an actor, producer, and writer, as well as much Barker-Gilbert Murray correspondence and some with other people. Concludes that Barker "never discovered himself." Has a useful list of characters played by Barker and of first performances of plays produced by him. Also contains a very complete bibliography (as of 1956) of Barker's writings in their various editions and of his unpublished works, the bibliography having been compiled by Frederick May and Margery M. Morgan.

Shaw, Bernard. *Bernard Shaw's Letter to Granville Barker*. Edited by C. B. Purdom. London: Phoenix House, 1956; New York:

Theatre Arts Books, 1957. Informative and often amusing letters written primarily during the years 1900–1913. The majority of them, written during the Vedrenne-Barker seasons at the Court, are full of Shaw's advice to Barker about his acting and producing, and give Shaw's views about various actors in relation to roles in his plays. Some of them reveal Shaw's high opinion of Barker's playwriting. A few deal with censorship, the national theater, the Frohman repertory season at the Duke of York's, and the Lillah McCarthy-Barker management of the Little Theatre.

———. "Granville-Barker, Some Particulars." *Drama*, n.s. no. 3 (Winter 1946), pp. 7–14. Same published as "Barker's Wild Oats." *Harper's*, January 1947, pp. 49–53. Important account of Shaw's friendship with Barker from beginning to end: Barker's first appearance as Marchbanks and their Court Theatre days, his marriage to Lillah McCarthy and their divorce, and Barker's second marriage, which resulted in his separation from Shaw. Also expresses Shaw's high opinion of Barker as a producer and a dramatist.

Storer, Edward. "Dramatists of To-day." *Living Age*, January 24, 1914, pp. 225–27. Perceptive comments on *The Marrying of Ann Leete, The Voysey Inheritance, Waste,* and *The Madras House.*

Sutton, Graham H. *Some Contemporary Dramatists*. London: Leonard Parsons, 1924, pp. 13–38. Sympathetic discussion of the plays, not including the one-act plays, collaborations, or *His Majesty.*

Taylor, John Russell. *The Rise and Fall of the Well-Made Play.* London: Methuen, 1967, pp. 112–15. Suggests that *The Voysey Inheritance, Waste,* and *The Madras House*, though intended as well-made plays, are not successful as such because the events are overwhelmed by too much talk, and that in his last two plays Barker moved toward subjective fantasy in works not intended for performance.

Trousdale, Marion. "The Question of Harley Granville-Barker and Shakespeare on the Stage." *Renaissance Drama* 4 (1971): 3–36. Traces Barker's idea that performance defines the dramatic text and questions how feasible this approach is for the scholar, or indeed whether this is true.

Whitworth, Geoffrey. *Harley Granville-Barker 1877—1946.* Reprint of a broadcast. London: Sidgwick & Jackson, 1948. A brief laudatory summary of Barker's career as an actor and a producer, with just passing mention of his work as a dramatist.

Wilson, A. E. *The Edwardian Theatre.* London: Arthur Barker, 1951, pp. 163—209. Places Barker in the context of the period, reviews and generally praises the Court Theatre venture, discusses briefly and favorably *Waste* and *The Madras House.* Quotes contemporary reactions to many plays (not just Barker's). Gives a useful account of the Censorship Inquiry of 1908 by a parliamentary committee.

Index

(Barker's works are listed under his name.)

Achurch, Janet, 2, 10
Actor, contribution of, 118
Admirable Crichton, The (Barrie), 34
Adrienne Lecouvreur (Scribe and
    Legouvé), 10
Aglavaine and Selysette (Maeterlinck),
    15
Alladine and Palomides
    (Maeterlinck), 89, 124
American Copyright Bill, results of,
    108
Anatol (Schnitzler), 7, 18
Androcles and the Lion (Shaw),
    7, 23, 24, 25
Antoine, André, 10
Archer, William, 2, 107, 110, 114,
    119, 120; comment on *The
    Marrying of Ann Leete*, 30, 49;
    comment on *The Voysey
    Inheritance, Waste,* and *The Madras
    House,* 49; comment on *The Secret
    Life,* 90
Arms and the Man (Shaw), 6, 17
Auden, W. H., 124
Audience, contribution of, 118

Back to Methuselah (Shaw), 89, 123
Baker, George P., 26, 107
Bancroft, Squire, 119
Barker, Harley Granville:
    ancestry, 1; appearance, 8; as
    Marchbanks in *Candida*, 3–4;
    association with Stage Society,
    2–3; autobiographical
    significance in plays, 81, 97–98,

100, 101; belief that writing
more important than producing,
132; characters in plays of,
102–103; characteristics as
dramatist, 99–110; collaboration
with Herbert (Berte) Thomas, 3;
compared with Barrie, 107; compared with Galsworthy, 16,
35, 56, 68, 104, 109; compared
with Henry James, 109; compared with Ibsen, 88, 104; compared with Shaw, 16, 35, 56, 68,
100, 103–104, 107, 108–109,
110; contributions as dramatist,
113–14; conversion to Socialism,
2; death, 8; evaluation of as actor,
6; first public appearance in a
play, 2; heroes in plays of,
100–101; heroines in plays of,
101–102; in New York, 7,
23–26; in World War I, 7;
influence as a producer, 14,
22–23, 28–29; influence on
repertory theaters, 17–18;
influences on, 107–110; lack of
popularity as a dramatist, reasons
for, 110; last appearance as an
actor, 7; management of Little
Theatre, 18; marriage to Helen
Manchester Gates Huntington,
7, 111; marriage to Lillah
McCarthy, 6; meeting with
Lillah McCarthy, 2; meeting with
Shaw, 2; "millionaires' theater,"
offer of, 16–17; parts played at